LEARNING FROM THE LEAVERS

Chats about Church

Local people share their thoughts and help us understand why they struggle to attend or have left their churches

Bret Tate

TABLE OF CONTENTS

This book is dedicated to my father who so generously gave of his time and resources to serve his Christian brothers and sisters without fear or favor. He did so without expecting any personal benefit, reward, recognition, power or position. I would have enjoyed hearing him being told:

'Well done, good and faithful servant!'

Acknowledgements

Thanks to everyone who has helped motivate, guide and correct me during the writing of this book.

Thanks to those who helped initiate my concerns about people leaving churches in our town and particularly to Pablo, who drew up a shockingly long list of men who had left our church in the period of just a few years.

Thanks to my wife, who patiently bore with my reluctance to get on with the project and my many and various excuses for delay.

Thanks, Mum, for your encouragement and constant prayer. It means the world to me and to quite a few of my friends that you so faithfully remember us before the Lord you serve with such joy and positivity.

Thanks to Jim Watchman, my good friend and prayer partner for many years, for proofreading the first full draft so diligently and suggesting really helpful changes.

Thanks to the folk at Amazon Publishing Pros for your patient proofreading and editorial expertise. It has been encouraging to see my project turn into a book.

And last but definitely not least, thanks to those 'local' people who were prepared to share their stories and sometimes their significant pain. Some of you have been my good friends for years, while others are only known to me through a church connection. I apologise to all of you for taking so long to share your stories and experiences with one another and others. Apologies also for using the rather impersonal term 'leavers' of you all. I tried several other descriptions but eventually settled on that term due to its neat description of the common experience underpinning this book. Thanks also to those of you who helped me turn the text into a more accurate and meaningful presentation through your suggestions and feedback.

About the Author

Bret Tate gained a B.A. degree in Theology from the London School of Theology where he was also awarded the Advanced Diploma in Pastoral Studies. With an enduring interest in education, he has spent most of his professional life working as a teacher, a school leader and a Special Educational Needs Adviser in England.

His M.A. in Education focused on 'Enabling Learning' and he is a keen advocate of giving a voice to stakeholders and of increasing the capacity of professionals and institutions to genuinely listen and hear more effectively.

In his first book, Bret draws attention to the experiences of church leavers, with an unusual focus on those who have left churches within one local area. In doing so, he encourages us to listen carefully to the voices of those who have left churches, in the hope that we can all benefit from **learning from the Leavers**.

Bret likes to spend his leisure time with his family and friends-trying to avoid injury while climbing trees, jumping rope and running about with his very lively grandchildren or kayaking with friends. He has promised his grandchildren that, with their co-authorship, his second book will explain, with many myths, how he lost his hair!

Introduction: Chats as Snapshots of Perception

Chats and Snapshots

Underpinning this book is a set of conversations with local people who share the experience of having left at least one church in our town. By 'local', I am referring to people who live in or near Upton (not its real name), the town in which I live and who attend, or have attended, churches in the same town.

I'm going to call the conversations we had 'chats' because they were personal but quite brief. I see these chats as snapshots of perception rather than records of systematic thought. I had the overall idea of 'learning from leavers' in mind, but I did my best to avoid steering the conversations too narrowly, allowing them to be 'unstructured' rather than based on a set of pre-selected questions. In that sense, the conversations were certainly more like chats than interviews.

There is a lot of explanation that could be covered at this point in order to set the chats in context.

There's the fundamental concept of learning from leavers, the methodology employed in the project and the contextual factor of my own personal and family experience. There is also the meanings and definitions of words—especially the word 'church' with its 'trip-up' terminology potential! (see the relevant section of Part 5 now if you are concerned about that in particular).

Some of you will want to read about those contextual factors before you read the 'chat' content and that is fine. You will find them explained in the appendix, which I had originally written as the introduction. However, I suspect most of you will appreciate getting straight into what our leavers had to say. For me, the priority is letting their voices be heard and learning what we can. In order to do that, all I need to do is briefly explain my use of anonymisation and pseudonyms and even more briefly introduce the structure of the book.

Why Did I Change All the Names?

There's an emphasis on genuine experience and authenticity in this book. Published material has been credited with original names, but I have changed the names of the people, the churches and the town involved. Either that or I have avoided using names in various places where the events from one reference could identify, for example, one church which would then identify it for other events. Anonymisation of this sort is an attempt to ensure that this book is a help and not a hindrance to both individuals and churches.

While it is valuable to know that the accounts you read are from genuine people in a genuine setting and that the quotations used are what real people have actually said, I've thought it wiser to avoid identification that could hurt individuals or relationships. I have searched my own motivation carefully over this and I do not think that this personal anonymity violates the important principle that it is the truth that sets us free (John 8: 32).

Despite this attempt at anonymity, some readers will be tempted to identify individuals and churches. For readers who were not involved in the chats, there may be some specific events that lead you to identify yourselves. If that is you personally, I ask that you allow yourself the opportunity to engage with what can be learnt by us all rather than give in to any temptation to sit in judgement over others or to feel personally applauded or criticised. There's every chance it wasn't about you anyway!

A Note on the Structure of This Book

This book is divided into five main parts. The first is the presentation of a selected focus from each chat. The second is a discussion of themes arising out of the chats. The third is a summary consideration of what we can learn. The fourth is a postscript giving an opportunity for leavers to comment further, having seen parts one to three and the appendix. Part 5 (the appendix, which started as the introduction so as to cause maximum confusion!) provides the background and context to the project as well as looking at how we use the word 'Church' or 'church'.

BRET TATE

LEARNING FROM THE LEAVERS

PART 1: SUBJECTS IN FOCUS

The Process of Identifying a Focus and Editing Chats

I have taken the liberty of trying to identify in each chat one subject that seems to present itself as more sharply in focus than the others covered. It isn't necessarily what was spoken of most, or even most forcefully, although that is true in some cases. It is more likely that it conveys a perception unique to that individual chat, not brought into that same sharp focus elsewhere.

The process of undertaking such a selection was initially my response to my concern about trying to shoehorn personal perceptions into a range of identified themes, even where these had been suggested through the set of chats. Part 2 takes up those themes and presents the opportunity to allow contributors to speak on subjects other than the one in sharp focus.

In addition to the selection of a focused subject, the chats recorded here have been edited with the purpose of retaining meaningfully, what was said by each contributor without unhelpful repetition, redundant expressions or identifications. My own contribution has been removed unless it is needed to give sufficient context to make sense of what the other person was saying. In this sense, for some of the chats, you are being presented more with what one person conveyed through it rather than the chat itself. There are some very obvious questions arising from this type of editorial inconsistency, but I hope you'll find that it doesn't undermine the power of each snapshot of perception.

Chat 1: Nigel and Patricia—Leaving Without Blessing

Nigel and Patricia are a married couple who left a church in Upton because they believed it was right to join one in another town that was not in the same denomination. They experienced a lot of pain in the leaving, not least because of fractured relationships and the sense that they had not been able to leave well and with the blessing of the church.

Patricia: *The thing I've found the hardest in moving on from church is that it's not just denomination to denomination. It's moving to the parts of the body where the Lord knows either that we are going to be fed or we are going to bless others and I think it's a really painful thing when you leave church with no blessing at all. I understand that sometimes people feel its rejection. It's really hard because it rocks your faith because you think, are we hearing the Lord correctly? But you know, you know when you hear his voice. In my experience, unless you're part of the leadership and you're leaving* *under the same denomination to something new—in that situation, people always seem to get blessed, but if you're just moving on because you know the Lord is starting to knit you together somewhere else, and it may be a different denomination, it's the Body of Christ, regardless of this denomination or that denomination or in leadership or not in leadership, because actually, we are all in ministry.*

Nigel: *From our experience, I think that was quite apparent, where if you're moving to a different denomination, it's quite apparent how the reaction or the leadership reaction is to you. It's unfortunate, but I think they think we may have failed the people at some point because they're moving on. But I also think it's quite possible that they could have a sort of entrenched mentality just to that denomination and they're not open to the bigger church body. I think there's definitely a difference in going to a completely different denomination. I also think, if you're not in the immediate circle of leadership, 'cause we've witnessed people in leadership moving on to different places for different reasons as well, not necessarily because they're moving from one side of the country to the other, but they've felt that they had to move, be it in a negative situation or not, but because they're established in leadership and they're sort of stalwarts of the* *denomination or whatever, then the reaction to them going is less negative as opposed to people that aren't in that immediate leadership group.*

Patricia: *...I think cliquiness in church will often drive people away, but you just have to learn, as Jesus did, to bear the offence and turn it to prayer and not to take things personally. But that comes down to your relationship with the Lord and how much you carry and about loving people as brothers and sisters in Christ. When you reject a Christian, then you are rejecting Christ in that person.*

Chat 2: Morris and Agnes—They Just Don't Care

Morris and Agnes experienced a great deal of pain in more than one church they attended. This seems to have been characterised by the lack of care and the failure of church leaders and others to live up to the expectations that are created by regarding the church as a family or a place to be surrounded by genuine friends.

Agnes: *I stopped going to a church about ten years ago, was it? And the reason I stopped was because I was doing so much that I burnt out and I didn't quite know how to deal with it, so I took a week off, which became two weeks, then a month, and then I began to realise that nobody was asking where I was even though I was on teams, and in meetings and present, making a contribution. So then it became about how long is it going to be before somebody knocks on my door and shows that they've got concern for my welfare. Actually it was a year and I didn't answer it because,* *by that point, that boat had sailed. That will be where it started for me. I'm not so bothered now about saying, 'No'. So in the place that I'm in currently, I've said I'll do something and then when I've felt like I need to stop, I've stopped. But I've noticed that when you're doing a job, it's almost like people notice you, but when you stop doing a job and you are just a member of the congregation, you become quite invisible. That's kind of my experience of church.*

Bret: *Invisible to who?*

Agnes: *Everybody, really.*

Bret: *Don't you have your own group of friends within the church congregation?*

Agnes: *Not really. I've got one or two people that I would consider friends…*

Morris: *But that's a retrospective thing, isn't it? Because actually, when you're in it, you think, yeah, I've got a circle of friends. I've got a circle of people who care, a circle of people who would be concerned. But it's when you're in a time of need and that circle is not there or bothered, then you think, Oh, I was wrong. So actually, I didn't have that circle of friends. Do you know what I mean?*

Agnes: *When it came to the moment when you probably needed people to come round for tea or ring you up, it wasn't the people you expected.*

Morris: *There were three people who I would say have actually been brothers in the faith. They've been good friends. Those three people who were concerned would actually seek me to see how I was. And actually, I would say those three people are more, I suppose, more Christian men rather than linked to that specific church, if you see what I mean. They kept me going, totally, both of us, wasn't it, really? But certainly, the leadership of the church, which I would have expected some sort of...*

Agnes (cutting in): *I even approached them.*

Morris: *You did. You were told, 'I don't feel I'm being called to come and talk to Morris.' and you think, 'Well, surely you're being called to shepherd your flock. Surely you're being called to minister to your church.' And it's not only that. I thought they were my friends. That has had a big knock-on now 'cause I have gone totally the other way and actually, I very rarely contact anyone— very, very rarely now. I've become quite reclusive.*

Agnes: *I think you start the whole church journey with an expectation. Maybe it's an expectation that the church can't actually fulfill. But the real church—how we relate to each other—those kinds of Christians are* *really rare, I think. People who say to you, 'Call me if you need me', and they really mean it.*

Morris: *I just think I don't want to be there anymore because I don't feel I belong. I don't feel I've got actual friends there who I thought I had. I want to go to church and worship God, but what happens is I go to church and I get cross and I get cynical. Then I feel guilty, and I get cross with myself. I come out and I just feel like a dreadful person, a dreadful Christian because I haven't been able to get with God because actually, I know I've got to forgive all of that stuff.*

You know, I've spoken to leaders in the church about how I feel. No one's ever gotten back to me on it. No one really appears to give a toss. The number of times you've (indicating Agnes) spoken to people at church and I think they've almost given up trying to say stuff to you now. There have been so many times when, 'Oh yeah, we'll do this, we'll do that, we want you to be involved in this or we want you to do this,' and then just throw you on the slagheap. They just don't care.

Chat 3: George and Scarlett—God Moves Us On

George and Scarlett were leaders in various roles at Bethany for many years. Their experience echoes that of numerous leavers who recognize the direction and calling of God in moving them on from a church as well as the difficulties and frustrations that were factors, on a human level, in deciding to leave.

Scarlett: *I think there's a blessing in us leaving. If I think back, my life is like a series of walled gardens. If I look back, it's been situational. I've been to different churches. It was time to leave one when the teaching was (indicates 'not good') and the church was cliquey. I went to the church in Dunder. It was at that church that George became a Christian. We were there for a time, then there was a split. We joined St. Stephen's. That was my cell group. That was my church—Wednesday evening, not Sunday morning… There would sometimes be just three of us and the Holy Spirit was just so powerfully present. It was amazing. We left again on* *that occasion. God told us we had to leave. That's very much how the Lord has grown me. We've had to learn new things. We've been at Bethany twelve years,. The Lord has been very gracious with us: moving us on.*

George: *It's got more difficult towards the end. Along the way, we've felt fully connected, but there's a total change in the end. When we first arrived, we just knew it was the right place. It's the same with leaving. There's that real conviction. It's time.*

Scarlett: *I remember shortly after Gavin left, I was thinking, how is this all going to keep going and the Lord pulled me up and said, 'Gavin is not the head of the church.' You don't mean to put anyone on a pedestal, but you think, 'How is this going to work?' It was a reminder that Gavin is part of the body. We are all part of the body with different roles. It's a bit like when God said to me with us moving. We are just having an L-shaped move. We are still on the board. We haven't gone anywhere, and God has moved us on in just a different way. We are all part of the chess game God is playing. What God does through us may be different, but we all have a role to play. I found that very helpful. Gavin under. Jesus is the leader.*

Scarlett: *I've said this to (a leader). God will bless us in leaving and they will be blessed in us leaving. God cannot bless where there is disunity. We have caused* *some disunity, so actually, by us no longer being there (with the) issues that we've had, it can take away a hindrance to the Holy Spirit. There have been people who can't look me in the eye and who would walk away from me. George says I give off 'the prickly look.' However, as a leader, you have to deal with those things and those people. I've had to do it and approach people and try to sort it out. That was not done by a few people, but before Sunday, I had some repenting and forgiving to do myself. I've had the opportunity to ask people to forgive me for the way I've behaved. I feel that I've drawn a line under that, but I feel us leaving will take away an aspect of hindrance so they can have unity.*

Chat 4: Jocelyn and Jayden—Zoning Out

Jocelyn and Jayden used to attend Upton Life Church, but following some personal and family issues, Jayden moved to another church. This was a smaller church where he felt relationships were more personal and it was possible to maintain closer connections. Jocelyn stayed at ULC, but she describes clearly the reasons for her feeling of zoning out.

Jayden: *One thing I have been aware of ever since my early Anglican days was that the bigger churches get, the more distant the pastor and leaders and the gap between the general congregation gets bigger. It doesn't mean they don't come down and chat with you, but when I go to my place of praise now, Salem church, I go along and if I'm down, someone wraps their arms around me. There's a feeling of community. ULC has grown. There's a feeling of us and them. It's to do with size. The church leadership has accommodated themselves to a different building. There's a distance, a* *definite distance which means when you're feeling low, the distance is hard to cross.*

Jocelyn: *I would see it differently. I don't think it's to do with size but to do with the culture of the church. When churches have a culture of everybody looking out for each other, if you're feeling fed up or miserable, then people would be looking out for you. You'd have connections with people who would notice things. As the church gets bigger, you can't know everybody, but if you've got connections with people, you know if the church is really good at connecting people regardless of who they are. At the moment, at ULC, I am zoning out. I do not feel particularly connected to the church. In my journey of discovery, I've been appreciating the shape that I've been made and I've been enjoying discovering the things that God makes you to do. It's not arduous. That's why I love my job. I'd do it even if they didn't pay me, I love it. To discover that servanthood is not burdensome. For me, actually, the things God has been leading me into, the conversations and the opportunities I've had outside of the church have been amazing. I've just been growing with God, and it hasn't been anything to do with the church. It's been appreciating seeing God in the every day and having great conversations with the patients and staff. That's been great, but that doesn't happen in church. I go and I feel frustrated.*

Going back to the zoning out thing... I went to the leadership about something. I was given advice that I chose not to do. Now I give the leadership a wide birth because regardless of whether they make an assumption or not, I feel judged because I didn't take their advice.

Once you're not part of the activities that are used to maintain the church, it's easy to feel that you don't have relationships. When you have a role or something to do, you have natural conversations about that, but when you stop the involvement, then it's easy to drift off.

Chat 5: Ben—Musical Mishaps

A number of years ago, Ben was a church music team leader well appreciated for his enthusiasm and commitment. When we chatted, he expressed some strongly held views about what has been happening to music and singing in his own experience and of some of the local churches he has attended. It seems, for Ben, as for numerous others, that music has the power to drive people away from church as well as to attract them to it.

As you know, I was a music team leader for a long time and singing and introducing new stuff from Spring Harvest, this was back in the late 80s that was good. Every Spring Harvest, you'd come back with two or three new songs, but it seems to have accelerated to such a stage now where there are new songs being written every five minutes and they are being taken on board willy-nilly almost.

Some places think everything always has to be new and you can't do anything traditional. By all means, have new stuff, but not everything needs to be new. At one church where I questioned it, the minister said, 'Oh no, no, we don't like doing anything that's more than about six months old. We like all the new stuff.' It made me feel they had a particular agenda for themselves rather than for the whole church, particularly when I spoke to an old man who's been going there all his life. We chatted about this man previously who stays out of the services because the music is so loud and repetitive. It always seems so sad when the stuff you were singing in the church a few years ago, you never hear nowadays—and it was good stuff. That's partly nostalgia, I realize.

I feel a lot of the modern music is vacuous—the words are vacuous, almost as though someone has cherry-picked phrases from biblical experience or something they've heard.

In many cases, they're not songs that can be sung by a congregation. They are performance songs. I used to enjoy Songs of Praise, but that's going the same way now. They have to put the subtitles on because you can't even tell what the words are... They need to be heard. But you quite often find that's not the case... everyone claps at the end. They see it as a performance.

The clapping. If you're clapping God, it would have words in it as well, rejoicing and hands up... This is just people clapping. I find that unhelpful. I'm not saying all clapping is wrong... you can clap Christian performers, but to have it in church just seems to be out of place to me.

A little example of that (performance element) was at Upton Hope Church at Christmas. They were singing a song that was banal... I got so disinterested that I was watching the bass player who spent the entire time looking down and fiddling with his instrument controls—on his thing on the floor, then on the amp behind him. It's not a very good example for people. You're looking at them and you get distracted.

I've got to the point where I'm coming out of the church and I'm so worked up in myself about things like that and it's nearly always the music...

Chat 6: Emilia—Leadership Behavior

Emilia has attended several local churches over the years, that we have known each other. I would characterize her as a very serious-minded and committed believer with a deep concern for the Biblical truth and prayer. Hers was the only chat that touched on an experience of denominational leadership beyond the local church, and I think it is worth sharing that within the context of her perceptions about the local church.

Emilia: *When (I was) first there, there was a lot of freedom to contribute, and I felt I could contribute something. I liked Gavin's teaching depth, so I was relatively happy. They moved from the school to the church building. We had a situation where Gavin was burnt out, but I don't think we knew about that. Then all of a sudden, one Sunday morning, Martin said he was going. Then there was an announcement that Gavin was going to take a break. That was a shock.*

Very soon after they announced that someone had been appointed to replace him.

Bret: *Who was the 'they?'*

Emilia: *Ernie Plant. He was meant to be an Apostle. I've had a lot of problems with Ernie. He used to lead a home group as part of the church. He decided to leave leading the group when he put a nineteen-year-old in charge. I had to say something, but he blasted me out of the room. He was so angry. My friend Dorothy was a witness to the state I was in.*

Bret: *Does the church get Ernie to come along and affirm the leadership?*

Emilia: *Oh, totally. I was asked to go to the prophecy evenings. I missed the first two. I went, but Ernie was talking about prophecy. I couldn't make head or tail of what he was saying. Then he said, 'If any of you don't submit to leadership, you can go out that door now.' We were shaking. We were in our seats like this (indicates fear). I should have got up and said something and walked out. That's what I should have done. We were quaking. There's a guy who had come with his disabled wife. She struggled with the level of noise in the music. They were told (by the leaders), 'We are not prepared to turn the music down.' I never saw him from that point until I happened to see him just before Christmas. I asked if he was going to another* *church. He said, 'No.' He'd prayed to the Lord about going back and the Lord told him not to go through the threshold of the building. That spoke to me. I've been very unhappy for a long time and very concerned because that's how God saw it. God cares about each individual. Would Jesus have said, 'You'll have to leave 'cause we've got to have the music that loud?'*

Bret: *But they've just recently said that one of their values is family.*

Emilia: *I find it very, very hypocritical, all the stuff they've been expounding... it doesn't fit in with my experience of them. I got the slides (on vision sharing) and I read them. Not true, absolutely.*

Chat 7: Garth And Yuna—Need To Be There?

Garth and Yuna shared their own personal experience of church through individual events. Yuna began by recounting how God had sent someone along to the church very specifically to speak to her. This was not someone from within the church but an unknown visitor. A number of years previously, Yuna had become a Christian, been baptized and attended the church but had left before returning years later. In our chat, she and Garth expressed different views about how necessary or important it is to attend church.

Bret: *Now, can I ask you about Sunday? We were both sitting upstairs and I saw you walk out. I thought, I wonder if you are alright because you had a rather determined stride on you.*

Yuna: *I got in there and something just didn't feel right that day. I thought I'll go sit upstairs and no one will see me there. The music started, but I didn't feel I could sing the songs. It was really odd. I have felt that* *before. I got up and stood outside and I thought someone will come and talk to me and I can talk it out with someone. No one came, so I got a bit upset. Arnold came out and ended up talking to a man who was also standing in the archway. I thought no-one's coming out to talk to me, so I went into the car park. I wanted to leave, but my car was blocked in.*

I rang Garth and said I just want to leave church, I can't do this, I feel so alone. I got off the phone. The signal was terrible. We were trying and trying to talk to each other, and I was texting and I thought. Oh, I'll just try and go back inside. Don't worry about it. The man that was hovering in the archway said, 'I hope you don't mind, I heard your conversation with your husband. Are you alright? Do you want to talk?' Then he just started talking and talking. I'd never seen him before, but he talked with such insight and with such wisdom it kind of felt a bit freaky. But I thought whenever you've had that freaky feeling before, it's been, God. Go with it, so I went with it. I gave him bare, minimal information about my life and he spoke into my heart and said, 'God loves you exactly the way you are right now. Not tomorrow when you've changed this. Not yesterday when you haven't done that. He loves you now.'

Bret: *And you'd never seen him before?*

Yuna: *Never seen him before. And the strangest thing happened; he said, 'I want you to walk down there. Go, get yourself a cup of tea and I want you to walk back and when you're on your way back, I want you to pray.' He said, 'I don't know what you're going to pray about 'cause I don't know your situation, but I promise you if you do as I've said, there'll be a gift inside that church for you from God.' And I'm feeling a bit skeptical and a bit weirded out with this whole thing. He walked me halfway. He told me he was from America and that God had told him to come to England for some reason and he doesn't know why but this might have been the reason.*

He said, 'I'm going to leave you here and you're going to go to that coffee shop and you're going to do exactly as I've said, okay? And don't look back.' I went there and I looked back when I got there. The car that was blocking me in was gone and he was gone, but it wasn't long enough for him to be able to walk back and get into his car and drive off without me hearing an engine go and it was—well, I'll have to go and get this cup of tea now. I'll have to pray on my way back. I wonder what it's going to be when I get into the church. I wonder if it's going to be anything. Maybe it's a crazy man or I'm hallucinating this whole thing. I went back in (to church) with my hot chocolate. I sat in the children's room… the speaker was quite loud, which made it strange. The way Philip was speaking, it was very piercing and the way I was sitting, Philip was framed perfectly by the window with the blue lights on him. He said, 'We need to stop telling people how bad they are and start telling them how good God is.' It brought me to my knees, and I was sobbing. And then he said, 'If anyone wants to feel the Holy Spirit, come up.' So I went up. Everybody seemed to link arms with each other. I was at the back and I wasn't in it. I stood there on my own while everyone linked arms and they'd blocked me out. I heard this voice say, 'Turn around and leave.' So I went to turn around to leave. Serenity grabbed my arm and pulled me into the center of the circle and I had a prayer like I've never had before. I had a release like I've never had before. And I spoke to a few people afterward, Martin Grant, I told him about what had just happened and what I couldn't work out and he said, 'That was an angel.'

Bret: *That's what I was thinking. Whether it's an angelic angel or God sending a person who obviously listens to him very closely, one or the other, it's clear that the Holy Spirit has led them, that person, to be there for you, which is really uplifting, isn't it, 'cause it shows how much God cares about you.*

Yuna: *It was all planned!*

Yuna's involvement with the visitor had a profound impact on her, and, as you will see, she felt it suggested support for her views about needing to be 'in church.' This, however, seemed quite different from Garth's experience of church and his focus on living out his faith outside the confines of church.

Garth: *I've gone to the 5 o'clock service, but I didn't get anything out of it. My work hours mean I'm not going to church at 10 in the morning. The 5 pm one is for youth. I'm not one for the songs at the start. I can't let myself go and join in. I can quietly take it in. On Sunday, I was at the youth service and then I went to town. I bumped into a group of teenagers, and they wanted me to buy them alcohol. I didn't, but I noticed the youth out there on the street. Then I went to the service just two minutes away. The bus (a previous outreach to young people in a local park) was in prime place at the park where young people were. There are always going to be places where they want to hang around together.*

Bret: *You have a heart for serving and for making a difference.*

Yuna: *But you need to be in church to put those ideas forward.*

Garth: *We sit down and have countless meetings. A (named) man at church tried to get things in place. In the end, I ended up going to the (community) Centre* *away from the church, but there's only so much you can do. Put yourself out there again and again. I've tried.*

Yuna: *You went to go up (during a church service) and talk on the microphone, but Philip wouldn't let you. He said, 'You've only been here a month. I don't know where you're at.' They need to see you consistently to have faith in you, to know that they can trust you and put responsibility into your hands. I've had to earn the trust of the church by being consistent. Going to this and to that. Volunteering for this and that. Now, I feel if I went to them with an idea about something, I feel they would respect me and they would listen to me.*

Garth: *I've been baptized a year. I just wanted to get on the mic and say how much things have changed. He was kind of like, 'What family? You've not been here.' So, all of a sudden, I'm not part of the community. It's like because I'm not coming all the time, I'm not part of the community now. I'd been up very late. My friend wanted to commit suicide and I was talking with him. But that's why it was of God in the morning that I wanted to share I was grateful I'd found this place where I was accepted. I base everything on the Kingdom of God and his righteousness and seek to go out and find and look.*

Yuna: *Yes, but you also need to come back to the base to renew yourself.*

Garth: *I feel I can be on that frequency of love and I'm doing things the ethical and righteous way. I've quit jobs in order to do the righteous thing.*

Yuna: *Yes, but you're not going to church. If I hadn't been there last Sunday, I wouldn't have had that revelation, would I?*

Yuna (to Bret): *My concern with Garth's attitude of, 'I'm doing God's work, but I'm not doing it within the church,' is that it could be perceived by others as he's just doing good, he's not doing good in the name of God.*

Garth: *But you're worrying about what other people are thinking. If you say you're a Christian, people have this prejudice against you. If you're doing good, why do you need to name it? With my work and day-to-day stuff. I'm helping kids learn and in my work, I want to be serving all the time. I like to be hands-on and throw myself into my work. Even when (at work) I'm more of a counselor and diffusing situations. That's what I think is important. We can read scripture and all that, but we can disagree about that. I might see something figurative rather than literal. My version of Christianity isn't like other people's. I like good honest, simple Christianity.*

Chat 8: Ruby—Communication Crisis

Ruby left the church several years ago following a range of incidents where she felt that poor communication revealed attitudes that she could not reconcile with her expectations of Christians and healthy church life. This found particular expression in the lack of support from church leaders and inappropriate communications about her home life during the breakup of her marriage.

I'm done with the foolishness... I'm not going to put up with people making me feel crap because of jealousy, insecurity and anything else. I don't want to be in this church. I can't respect myself if I stay here with my feelings about those particular things. That was why I had to leave.

I know we can excuse bad behavior, but you know I'm done with the church in excusing bad behavior... if you go by Biblical principles, there is only one option. You go to that person if you've got a problem with them, then you go up to leadership. Well, it's like teaching. You go to the teacher. If you don't have any luck, you probably go to the head of the year. You go to the head and then failing that, you go to the board of Governors, then the school board of education. That's protocol. It's exactly the same as it should be in church.

When leadership found out that we'd broken up, we were still going to church. Nobody in three months talks to us and indicates this is a bit odd or weird. Who cares? Anyone? Is the captain aboard? I'm on the Marie Celeste. Nobody's home.

Imagine this situation. A couple has broken up. Leadership knows about it, and when I say leadership, they all now know about it, you know, the glorious inner sanctum. They know, but nobody has come to either of us and said, 'How's it going? Do you need any support? Do you want to talk about it? How is it with you both going to the church? How is that working for you? Is there anything you both need? Is there any area for prayer? I mean, I've been going to church for forty-eight years. I know what you need to do.'

Do you know, I'm not so much hurt as just fed up with the church now. It's not anger, it's disbelief. I'm in shock. I just don't get it. I think if I could reconcile it in my head... but I just don't get it.

You get more at the workplace. I'll be really honest with you. My non-Christian friends have been so supportive throughout all of it. They are forward. They will say how they feel and they are the first to ring up and say, 'I've remembered you've got this or that.' My Christian friends—there seems to be an inability to— well, no one wants to talk about the elephant in the room. It's all very uncomfortable, so they'd rather not.

Chat 9: Steve And Evelyn—Organic Or Manufactured?

Steve and Evelyn head up a missional community group linked to St. Stephen's Church in which they have seen encouraging numerical and personal growth in the group. Their experience of moving from one church to another and a period of overlap has influenced their views about the nature of church.

Bret: *You were experiencing something of Christian life in two different churches or two congregations. Do you now see St. Stephen's as your home church?*

Steve: *Yes, I got baptized there, which had been a big tie for me and then being put into leadership. I've always been fond of ULC because that's where I came to faith and the people who helped me out, like Henry.*

Evelyn: *No, I felt really guilty when I was trying to make the decision to move. I felt I was out of line. I didn't want it to be about what I could get from church. There were people who questioned me about church hopping. I spoke to mum about it and she was really helpful. She* *said if you're in a church where God is, you will get what you need. I hadn't felt that for a while at ULC. It had lost its heart a little bit. What it was when I started was a bit rough around the edges, but you knew God was there every Sunday. But there were more political things that happened at the time when we moved from the school to the church building: it somehow affected the nature of the church. It was a lot harder to connect to God. It morphed from something really organic to something really manufactured.*

Bret: *Really interesting choice of words. 'Manufactured' implies a sort of production line, tooled according to a certain fashion, made according to the plan, goes down the line and comes out as you planned it, but it's a process that is not organic. Organic things take their own way. They follow their nature.*

Steve: *That's not to say that planning is bad. I've noticed that personally, we like much more the organic side of things. The only thing we struggle with at St. Stephen's is that a lot of things are planned. That's what I missed the most at ULC. Sometimes you weren't even sure it was a church service.*

Evelyn: *We have a girl in our community who has had a really rough time. She's only 19/20. It's been horrible for her. Something she found very hard was coming back to church because so many bad things had* *happened when she was still at church. She expressed this and I said if you need to be somewhere else, that's okay. She now goes to Whitney Church, which she is really enjoying. She loves it, but she still comes to our group during the week. The dynamic is different and that's okay. It meant I had to find the church that was right for her.*

Steve: *I think our community could run as a church. The leaders kind of want that. One of two things can happen. More (outreach) communities or a church plant. There have been other church plants from leadership but not something like what we are suggesting.*

Evelyn: *We do a good job of running it. If we said everything was fine all the time, they would know something was wrong. They have continued input and we have that accountability.*

Bret: *What would their reaction be if people came to the meetings you have, but church attendance was affected?*

Steve: *That already happens. Sometimes we have more non-Christians than Christians in the meetings because we are getting the word out there.*

Chat 10: Ralph—All Change?

Ralph left St. Valarie's, the church in which he had served on the leadership team, sometimes as a preacher. He had moved to a newer church in the town, but at the time of our chat, he was taking an extended time out. His own relationship with the church seemed to be affected by the changes in his own thinking rather than the church changing.

Where I am now is not attending. I'm enjoying the Sunday morning peace and quiet while Bee goes off and does all the hand-waving. I came to a conclusion for a variety of reasons that I wanted to take some time out. I still believe and see myself as a Christian. I still pray. I have a strong, if convenient to me, faith. I still see myself as a member and part of the church. I go on high days and holidays, but I don't want to be there on Sundays. I'm still in fellowship with a lot of people. With King's Assembly, you always have people that are in and people on the fringe—part of the community but not necessarily the church.

Bret: *In that thinking, was there an unspoken expectation that the movement would be toward going into the church?*

Ralph: *In the early days, it was a church for people who had given up doing church. I'm a sort of fringe member.*

Bret: *So you've moved the other way, really?*

Ralph: *Yes, I used to live in the holy bubble. I was very involved and in the diaconate. I was preaching—I was a grade 2 preacher in the (name of a denomination) church. In the end, it was all becoming more and more meaningless. No, that's too strong, I felt like a square peg in a round hole.*

Bret: *What characterized that feeling? What changed?*

Ralph: *I can answer that, I think. It was about transitions. There are several things going on. The honest answer is me—that's what changed. Was it that or that the church didn't change? You went every Sunday morning, and it was the same old thing—whether (name of a denomination) or King's Assembly. It meets lots of people's needs, but to me, it was utterly predictable. First, we'll do this, then we'll do that. For me it was, what am I doing here? I was rebuilding motorbike engines in my mind. I didn't hear a word of* *the sermons because I was so switched off. I just felt I couldn't stay any longer.*

Chat 11: Nathan—Church As Addictive Business

Nathan had visited ULC a few times with his disabled wife. He had found the music very loud to the extent that his wife could not cope with it. After a couple of conversations with the senior leader about this and some other matters, he left the church believing that God had told him not to attend again. Nathan's experiences seem to have confirmed for him that church is more a business than anything else and one that exerts an addictive power over those who subscribe to it.

Nathan: *I wasn't there (ULC) very long and it's not right to comment on what other people have said about it. I think it is a job for him (the senior leader). It's a job. He's there to serve the people, as are all the elders but in my case, or my wife's case, he didn't. Could he not offer to come and pray with her?*

Bret: *What if he offered to pray—would that have changed your view of him?*

Nathan: *Yes, but I would also have wanted to challenge the need for the music to be so loud. If it's not in the Bible, we don't need to be doing it.*

Bret: *Has your view been confirmed regarding ULC that it is part of the 'system?'*

Nathan: *It's a business. It's a business because we pay the CEO, they have a building fund.*

Bret: *But it's not just money that establishes a business, the early church had money troubles. That's why they appointed the deacons. Would you say they were a business?*

Nathan: *I've not seen it in action—funds going to widows or people who need support. It goes to the clubs or the business's money pot for future plans. The business is focused inward, isn't it club, business, system? Very worldly! My whole outlook is different. I'm part of the church, so are you.*

Bret: *Do you have feelings of loss or being cast adrift or not belonging, whatever the theology?*

Nathan: *We must not go off feelings. When I first stopped going (to another church) decades ago, I had pangs, but they went away, the Lord provides someone to meet with. Well, before I came to Upton, I had no pangs. It's like coming off a drug. If you stop going, you feel bad. It's like an addiction. People feel bad if they* *are not there, but it's worldly. They haven't understood what the scripture is telling us about meeting together.*

Bret: *Sometimes people say they miss worship or singing. They feel they have not felt able to replace that in many cases. What's your reaction to that?*

Nathan: *I'd say buy a CD.*

Bret: *People would say that's not the same.*

Nathan: *You can praise God walking along the street. A lot of what they are missing is worldly. They are missing the music group at the front. It's because It's such a big change. It's like giving up sugar. You don't like it at the start, but you can get used to drinking tea without it and without sweeteners. The music group is another worldly invention of man. Music may draw unbelievers in and get more money in the coffers. It's a business.*

Bret: *What would the church need to do to show it is not a business after all?*

Nathan: *Apart from going bankrupt, they would say, 'Has God really told us to build this massive church?' and go back to putting the money aside for supporting the needs of others. You and I both know that won't happen barring God's intervention.*

Chat 12: Julian—Evangelical Certainty

Julian became a Christian at St. Stephen's church. He left the church at least in part due to his philosophical and theological views diverging from the evangelical expression of that church's beliefs and the *'dogmatic and intolerant'* certainty of what he saw as the typical evangelical perspective.

If I'm personally honest, I find nearly all of the evangelical church dogmatic and intolerant. That's not where I came from. I have an evangelical church background. Although I learned a lot about the Bible, we were destined to part because I'm a very liberal-minded person. You have great respect for different points of view and you don't just shut people up...

Here is a good phrase I got from (a friend at St. Stephen's), 'Surely He is a God who loves to hide himself.' (The friend) would chuckle, 'That's because he wants to give us the joy of finding Him.' The prophets speak of seekers, not like the evangelicals who have all the answers but joyful seekers on a journey. When we were in Chichester Cathedral, there was a lady with a grown-up disabled daughter who was being very loving. But her daughter was becoming restless, so the mum gently removed her. God was not in all the flim-flam and ritual. At that moment, where was God?

I like traditional worship. As CS Lewis said, it kind of works best when you know all the steps. We like traditional styles and others prefer other things, but we all have to be careful not to take ourselves too seriously. When I was at St. Stephen's, I liked to say, 'Great is the mystery of faith.' You can't encapsulate a mystery in a rule book.

The Proclaimers (A Scottish Folk duo) put it well: 'I believe in God all right. It's folk like you I just can't stand. You don't have to try to scare me to reinforce my faith, sir. 'Cause I believe someday, I'll stand before my maker and when I do it will be before the author and not some interpreter of his words.'

The popularity of the Dawkins and Hitchens cohort has grown, and religion should be able to take it on the chin. Hitchens tears Mother Theresa and others apart. His last book 'Mortality' was written while he was dying of cancer. I often prefer atheists to Christians because they are more honest. I admire the French existentialists because there was an immense sincerity in what they wrote based on saying, 'God is dead, what do we do?'

I think it was Plato who said that Philosophy is about learning to die well—in a way that's very true. The Victorians were better aware of death. One eulogy said, 'She lived in remembrance of her death.' Death gives a perspective to life. There's nothing wrong with enjoying what God gives us at this moment. I'm conscious I won't always have what I have now. Jesus said, 'Life is to be lived in its fullness.' There's no contradiction in fully enjoying life and caring for others too.

Chat 13: Aaron—Apostate Church

Aaron and I have enjoyed numerous chats about the nature of the church, the translations of the Bible, the pagan roots of various church practices and other theological issues. He used to be very regular in church attendance a number of years ago and was regularly involved in leading music ministry. Then he had an experience that radically transformed his Christian life and his views about the church.

Aaron: *Charles Newbold brings it out very clearly. The established church and union of the organized church with the state always go wrong. The quiet pilgrim church has kept to the original way and would not join the established church.*

Bret: *Most of these groups would still have wanted to use the word 'church.' We can't seem to get away from it. When considering the damage of the institutional church, people still want to use the word 'church.'*

Aaron: *If you just change it for another word, it's not helpful. I don't believe that's helpful. We have to understand it. We have to look at the history from the New Testament and, first of all get that established and say what was it supposed to be. Eldership is an important aspect of this and the false doctrines of the church and its amalgamation with paganism. Every time the church is institutionalized, it becomes a target for the government and this has happened over and over again. The true church has no buildings. Elders are seniors, not rulers. That true church always ends up getting organized.*

Tyndale's Bible comes along, then the King James (Bible). It was corrupted. They purposely changed it in the area of church and authority. The changes in the King James Bible reflect a pagan word church which Tyndale didn't do. He used 'congregation,' but he understood what it should have been. Most of the KJV is Tyndale's Bible, but they doctored it so there would be no revolution. The clergy had to be raised up and acknowledged. The key for England was that moment when the King James Bible came. It retained the term 'church' and the Anglicans took this on. Ekklesia is very at odds with that.

What do we go to church for? We say we go to worship. For those who have jettisoned the thing called church and for whom the meeting place has become anathema, that's not worship. There's a sort of pressure, even in an open environment, to follow a formula and a ritual. It's like a slide. We are continuing to slide towards a tradition and a form.

Bret: *Surely some formality is good, isn't it? Paul gives a form of order in I Corinthians that is formulaic. Someone has to put some order into a meeting in order to get it sorted at all.*

Aaron: *We want ekklesia. We want to be the church, not do the church. He (Jesus) is building the church. I really believe the key is to understand Rome. The marriage of paganism and the organized church. Constantine was pagan and was the first one to stop persecuting Christians, but he was not for the simple faith that Jesus started. He got a simple faith and organized it with pagan names knocked out and Christian names put in their place. We have paganism dressed up. The true church has lost many as it descended into the institutional man-made church. True believers break away from that again and again. The institutional church is man-made.*

A key passage is Revelation 17, where John sees the woman riding the beast. He was astonished. He was astonished because it was the institutional church. It goes further than that. He was astonished because it was what we call Christianity. We think as long as we use the word Jesus then the problem must be outside of that, but to grab the idea that the apostasy is within the church—that's what Satan would do. If I was Satan, that's what I would do. I would confuse people with false translations, so they don't know what to believe anymore. Then I would work my way into the church.

Chat 14: Josh and Kaylee—Giving and Doing Too Much

Josh and Kaylee left ULC, the church they had made a home in Upton. They were both very committed to the church in giving financially and of their time and energies in many ways, including taking up leadership roles for various activities. Their story at the church echoes that of many who find a level of interest and engagement from leaders at the church that fails over time. Characteristically when this is accompanied by high levels of giving and activity, it seems to lead to feelings of being used as expendable resources and emptied of value.

Josh: *The lesson learned is too much over-immersion, throwing everything at ULC. This started about the time Jacob started. He was very encouraging—lots of communication and really connected and helpful. It all began really well. That's the beginning of the journey and getting involved in all* *sorts of things. The whole start was really good. I had been asked to do lots of things like fundraising and then got drawn into the worship band.*

Kaylee: *And Jacob had a thing about being excellent in everything we do.*

Josh: *Yes, it was about the pursuit of excellence. It was all really good positive resonating stuff for us. There were requests for all sorts of other things. We did kids' work as well, but the fundraising thing started to compromise my work. I was doing lots of things and took on loads of responsibility, but it was like, 'Yes, and…' For me, there were signs along the way that my initial enthusiasm had been misplaced. Then there were a lot of changes like in the men's work. Many positive things started to disintegrate.*

Kaylee: *Was there a pivotal moment when you felt 'that's not for me?' You said there were lots but was there one point?*

Josh: *There was the personal side of me putting in hours, learning the songs so that I could turn up on Sunday knowing them. Then songs would be dropped, there was no time to practice other songs, and people would turn up late. That whole process, I felt, was really disrespectful. I was trying to do my part in this pursuit of excellence and it was actually a waste of time. I found it quite a pressure to play in the band, so that* *was my first action—to withdraw from the worship band.*

Then there was the financial thing. Amongst all of this, as a congregation, we were asked to increase our giving. This was to fund the new building, which came out of the blue, doubling our tithing or making a more significant contribution. We prayed about that. It was a big sacrifice and I think If I had that money right now, I'd be a bit more comfortable. We believed it was the right thing to do, but then to see what happened at the time when Philip was appointed as a new (leader) and he got that brand new car. We don't know how it all worked out, but it didn't sit well. You are seeing the leadership with their cars and bikes and houses, and it led me to question the thinking about what's behind some of this.

Bret: *There's a sense in what you say about value. In terms of the commitments you made, that initial connection had a sense of real value, but that is what followed less so.*

Josh: *It is some of that. Over time I just felt used. I felt I was just a resource. Just used, used.*

Bret: *You got to that point. You are a couple. What was going on with Kaylee while all that was happening?*

Kaylee: *I took longer because I was desperately trying not to leave. We talked about it at night, in the morning, praying about it, talking to people, consulting people who we greatly respect, leaders of churches in other countries. It was not what we wanted to do. I know that there's no such thing as a perfect church and that you just find different problems in different churches because life is messy. Human beings are messy. No (leader) is perfect. We wanted to be generous and be outpouring. We wanted to be a blessing. By God's grace, we are standing where we are. Looking back, it's been a lesson. I just threw myself into everything. I was very hospitable. I led women's Bible study - the worship. I got a real sense of passion for God when we were at the school and experiencing that passion and I loved that.*

Then we got a new leader. It started off well. He was after excellence in all things, and I thought, yes, I like that. Josh and I have various skills that work well together. There were some lovely people, godly people who walked alongside us, but there were others who just wanted more. I did the Christmas service, got the children involved and all that, but there was a disconnect. I met with Jacob to say we were running on empty. We were giving from emptiness and our experience of God and spiritual health comes increasingly from outside the church and we are not where we want to be. It just seemed to go over the top of his head. At the end of the conversation, he said something about taking up the kid's work. I thought, Jacob, did you not understand what I just said? We don't want to do more, we want to do less. We are struggling here. He doesn't seem to understand the spiritual journey, spiritual health, and growth. For me being part of the worship team was a very painful experience. There was no communication, no liaising, and no teamwork. I think the pivotal moment was when the leader turned up forty minutes late. He didn't say hello to me as usual. I got angry—it was the most horrible experience to be part of a worship team and feel angry. I wanted to run out of the building. I should have done it. The disrespect, the rudeness, the lack of kindness. The teaching was getting less, the music longer, and the congregational involvement was getting less and less.

(I had) a few anecdotal conversations with people. I was praying for a sign, but I felt, in retrospect, he (God) was putting people in my daily life who were telling me things about what went on. They were saying things about the church that made me think, 'What!' I thought about who I respected in the church, but I came up with only two people who I thought were sincere and humble

and desiring growth in their lives, well, three, actually. One is still in the church, one is hovering and one is about to leave. We met with Jacob. We said we've made mistakes and set ourselves up for the disappointment that leadership would be interested in our spiritual journey. He didn't flinch or show any real interest. Just said thanks for telling him.

Bret: *You describe something very similar to Josh, really. Lots of reasons and a journey of disappointment and overload, especially for those who have been in leadership. Did anything really change with what the church did or was it a change of perception on your part?*

Kaylee: *We thought the church would be kind and generous and open. I worked hard to make a connection. We dropped everything for all sorts of people. Is it the church that changed or us that changed? I think it's a combination of both. We became less. There's no connection, no depth and wisdom. It just became more and more clear that if we are going to grow, it's not going to happen in the church.*

Josh: *I increasingly left church on Sunday morning feeling worse than when I had gone in. I knew this was not God's plan for my spiritual growth—to come out of the church and feel rubbish.*

Kaylee: *I'm just going to concentrate on breathing and getting back to basics. I had a powerful revelation from God on Saturday. I feel he says we have made absolutely the right decision and we must be much more judicious about who we place ourselves with. Make your life fruitful! Be prepared to take a risk but don't rush into anything. Take your time! We fill our hands and God can't fill them. Carry on and grow! I think it's a question of time. Both of us will be led to different pastures, I'm not even thinking about that now; I need to personally understand the lessons I've learned.*

Chat 15: Declan—Decisions, Decisions

Chatting with Declan revealed his significant concerns about the church's decision-making. This particularly related to how leaders make decisions and although this was within the context of a single denomination, it may well reflect the experience of attenders and leavers in other denominations too.

Declan: *I've been with the church for ten years. I don't know where it went wrong. For me personally, I guess the gradual realization that what was happening in the church wasn't what I thought should be happening—it didn't seem right.*

Bret: *Just to clarify—you are still in the church. You haven't left?*

Declan: *I'm on the edge. I saw that email on Monday night about leadership. It was almost the last straw. I thought that's it. I wanted to reply to Jacob on that. I wanted to ask, 'Why has the church decided to change its views after a hundred-odd years?' It's not just that. It's the way it's done. The hierarchy and the way* *decisions are made within the church, both locally and nationally. This is a national decision that's been made by the church denomination without any reference to the membership.*

Bret: *Can you give me an example of where there has been decision-making that you think is inappropriate?*

Declan: *Well, buying that building, St. Valarie's Church. We were given a prophecy right back, ULC was given it before I joined, that the Lord would provide land and he did, totally debt free. It's all paid for. The buildings were all renovated, with church people helping out. It was very good. It was excellent and we had the space to build—well, we had the space but not a lot of money. We might have had the money if we hadn't spent it on St. Valarie's. It is a personal thing, but I know others in the church do share my feelings… about leadership. It was Gavin's idea. It was a knee-jerk reaction. He acted like I do when I see a new car— don't care how much it costs or who gets hurt—I'll have it! It was a big decision that I felt was not right.*

Bret: *But what would have been different about coming to a decision in a different way, though? Are you suggesting that they could have actually put it to the church in a different way and not been just a leadership decision?*

Declan: *Well, maybe, but the (name of denomination) doesn't act that way. It's not democratic. You can do it. The (name of another denomination) do it…*

Bret: *But the evangelical way is not really democratic. It's theocratic…*

Declan: *When you get to financial situations in the church, like buying St. Valarie's, there's a lot of money that comes into the church. A lot of people give a lot of money. It's not a Megachurch, but it's big from where we are. The decisions as to how that money is spent are airy-fairy. It wouldn't last five minutes in a business. It's the decision-making. The (leader) might say, 'Well, I think we need to buy so and so,' and that's it. Is the money well spent? I don't think so. I feel what's really missing is the accountability of the leadership to the membership. It should be there. I'm happy down there on Wednesday coffee mornings, but even that's changed. We're losing coffee morning. It used to be one morning a week when we used to get down there and sit around a big table and have a good laugh and a chat. We can't do that anymore. It's like they have taken something away from us.*

Bret: *I don't suppose you were involved in the decision to change that?*

Declan: *No, not at all. Philip and Jacob made the decision. And we can go back and look at things like the men's group that was terrific a few years ago. We couldn't get enough chairs. Everybody wanted to come. It was really good and then leadership got involved!*

Chat 16: Max—Leaving the Faith

The chat with Max was deeply theological but focused on his experience of leaving the Christian faith. For him, this momentous decision centered not on the behavior of others in the church or their treatment of him but on theology and personal belief. Nevertheless, the impact this had on important relationships and the personal pain involved is all too clear.

Max: *I tell you, every time I've had to leave a church, it's such a painful experience. I always feel like I'm turning my back on people. I can't say anything bad about the people. No one treated me badly at either church or Upton Hope Church. It was never about the people. I always thought that if you are a young Christian man, unmarried, you haven't got much of a chance. That's one of the reasons I went to (another country)—to find a wife, and I went to the (name of a denomination) church and there were loads of people* *my age dating and I enjoyed being with my peers. It was great and again, no problem with anyone there either, but I lost my faith at that point. I was there at that church for three months and I was a faithful church member. I had a nice time there. I went twice a week. I was friends with the (leader). They were nice people. When I lost my faith and I left the church, I had no friends and my boss was the only person that I could be friends with.*

Bret: *It's certainly not been an easy option for you. There's been a cost involved—to leaving the churches and then leaving your faith and that particular church at the time.*

Max: *They were angry because they thought I was trying to destroy other people's faith. I posted a video on a youth/young adults page on WhatsApp saying why I was leaving and one of the leaders was very angry and it was taken down straight away. He said I was trying to destroy other people's faith. They calmed down eventually because I was arguing with them outside the church and I was really upset. I was in a really bad place. I was totally lost. He did calm down and his wife came out and said, 'Do you want to come in? I really wanted to go in and eat with them and fellowship with them, but I just knew that I had to leave.'*

Bret: *Why did you post that video?*

Max: *I was friends with all these people—I just wanted to be transparent about it. I didn't want anything to be done in secret. I thought it would be better to get it out in the open and whoever was interested could tap me up, basically. It was a twenty-six-minute video that was only up for a minute. I had people asking me for the whole video. People were saying, 'I've got doubts too.'*

I'd had several meetings over about a month about the eternal punishment of Hell is what I was talking a lot about and what was on my mind. It was the next morning that I really left the faith. My boss was away. I drove to work and I cried while I was driving. I was really upset, and I wondered what would happen. Would I go back to the faith? What would I do now? I was in a real state. My mind was all over the place. My whole worldview had been shattered. I had no opinion on anything. I didn't know what to think of anything because everything was interpreted through a Biblical lens...

Bret: *And because you thought—by nature, you need that coherence?*

Max: *Yes, yes, I'd operated in that system— everything I thought and said...*

Bret: *So it was like dominoes falling?*

Max: *Yes, In my own mind, if I strayed outside my own standards, based on the Bible, if I wandered outside of that, I'd be very hard on myself, very hard, very harsh, like mentally tormenting—of being like a hypocrite or not, not being good enough. There was a meeting at the church that evening and I didn't go. And when I posted the video that was during the thing— while the service was going on. When it was removed, I was fuming. I was furious—they seemed so threatened by what I'd said. At that time, I was really fragile as well, and I felt like I knew what he (the leaders) thought like I was doing the work of Satan. He was very protective of the people in the church. I could tell that, and it was a kind of strange situation because I knew his mindset… I knew that I could not persuade him, and I really felt like the bad guy. I felt very upset by that 'cause I felt like, obviously, I loved and respected him, and he thought I was betraying him and trying to damage the faith of the people at the church. It's not what I was intending. I didn't intent to damage their faith, but then I sort of realized that they were like brainwashed. I mean, that's what I really thought. They've been tricked. I can see now what's been going on and I think that they should have the opportunity to hear what I have to say.*

You talk about the fullness of life, though. My life is so much better now that I'm not a Christian. I love my life now, and it's not just about me participating in sin or whatever. You might think, oh, he can do whatever he wants. That's what (a friend) said the other day. She said, 'Oh, you just want to join in with the sins of this world.' I enjoy just having a normal relationship with other people: not having to worry about whether they are going to burn in Hell forever. To just look at a person and think, yes, you're a nice person. Have a nice day. Do you know what I mean? Not, Oh, you need to believe the gospel or you're going to burn in Hell, and think that they're nice, but they are going to burn in Hell.

Bret: *You see, that's why I have trouble with that doctrine. I think it must affect every conversation you have.*

Max: *It does. It does.*

Bret: *But... but... plenty of Christians don't think that way, so it's not an inevitable outcome just of being a Christian.*

Max: *Here's the thing, though—I know if I go and rob a bank what will happen to me when the justice system hits me. I'm going to be put in jail, but no one has been able to prove to me that Hell (or) heaven even exists. No one can prove that an angel exists, or a devil exists, or a seraphim exists or... or any of it. It seems so harsh* *that people should come up against a punishment that they don't really know whether it's going to happen to them or not, especially when there are a bunch of other religions, also claiming to be the one true religion. Why should any person choose between Christianity and Islam? Why should any person that's a Hindu become a Christian? There's no reason. There's no real evidence.*

Chat 17: Dominic—Feeding the Faith

I'm sad that I can't use any direct quotations from Dominic. He died before I was able to secure his explicit permission to be quoted, but I wanted to honour his memory by including a reference to the chat we had together.

Dominic had attended a number of churches in Upton and, at the time of our chat, considered himself a member of Good Shepherd Church. He admitted he struggled to attend on a Sunday morning but enjoyed the fellowship that he had at church events such as the outreach coffee mornings.

What stands out from our chat is the benefits Dominic saw in a range of church activities feeding his faith. He was very honest about the difficulties he had 'connecting' at times in formal services, but he also recognised that being drawn into corporate fellowship and worship built up his faith and made him more aware of spiritual matters and the presence of God in particular.

It is also worth noting the contrast Dominic drew between his experiences of different churches in the town. In some, he had felt alienated and rejected by leaders, but he expressed a genuine appreciation for the support he had received from the leaders of Good Shepherd Church during a period of great personal difficulty.

PART 2: SHARED THEMES

The process of identifying and presenting shared themes

I identified themes while reading through the chat transcripts and by logging each apparent reference to the increasing number of themes as they presented themselves through that reading. The selection was not based on any themes or commonalities identified by other writers through their diligent research, so I make no claim to be rigorously addressing issues raised by anyone else. I also acknowledge that my own pre-existing notions of the themes that might emerge—my bias—cannot be ruled out.

In some ways, the lack of objectivity in theme identification mirrors the personal nature of my selection of leavers for the chats. I did not deliberately select people who had negative or painful experiences in leaving churches, but neither did I deliberately seek out leavers who had been very content with their own experiences in the churches they had left. For these and other related reasons, I can only offer this section as a tentative presentation of themes that readers might find interesting and that might spark further thought. I've tried to provide very limited theoretical perspectives from my own reading and thinking because it is the quotations from leavers that will be the major source of learning rather than my editorial links. I have included thoughts from some other sources where I thought additional light from outside would be helpful in providing a broader context.

As you read through the themes and leavers' quotations, you are likely to ponder why I included a quotation under one particular theme heading rather than another where it would seem more appropriate. My links are tentative and, as noted, serve only to contextualize the quotations. The quotations are the substance.

Theme 1: Hurt and Pain

Since we are his children, we are his heirs. In fact, together with Christ we are heirs of God's glory. But if we share his glory, we must also share his suffering. Yet what we suffer now is nothing compared to the glory he will reveal to us later.

Romans 8:17-18

For you have been given not only the privilege of trusting in Christ but also the privilege of suffering for him.

Philippians 1:29

The Pain of Staying or Leaving

All serious Christians know that God's call on our lives and experience involves suffering, but what takes many of us by surprise is the amount of pain and hurt that can be experienced at the hands and by the attitudes of those who we think of as brothers and sisters in Christ.

Let us be under no illusions. For most church leavers, the experience of leaving has been intensely painful. For some, the pain was all in the period prior to leaving and it was resolved and healed by leaving, but that doesn't seem to be the case for most. The more common experience is a long period of emotional and psychological discomfort both before and after leaving, often accompanied by unresolved resentment or the struggle to forgive the hurts experienced and to move on.

Patricia: *We've had to work through a lot, you know, forgiveness and also disappointment. You know, the things that go on in church just bring so much disappointment and it makes your heart sick.*

The pain that leads to leaving seems rarely to be based on a single incident and is much more often caused by a cumulative build-up of events that form a pattern. Nathan describes this as a set of contributory factors:

Nathan: *It was a combination of things happening, be it from minor decisions made by leadership to being talked to in a certain way on occasions... I don't think you can pin it down to one thing. In our experience, it was a sequence of situations or circumstances that led to that. It wasn't just, 'Oh, we can't possibly stay here cos the teaching's rubbish.' That wasn't the case. It was a contributing factor... It could be anything. It could be from how flippant the preacher would be one particular morning to coming forward with something to share that you strongly felt and not being allowed to share it, just little things like that contributed over a period of time.*

Declan similarly recognized a number of factors that caused him concern:

Declan: *In the last year or so, I have been seeing things happen in the church that I don't like—the way people are being treated, the music and some cranky theology.*

It is commonly reported by leavers that they experienced an extended period, prior to leaving, of increasing discomfort not just with what was happening externally but with how it was affecting them internally too:

Kaylee: *I admit that I felt resentment and anger... I don't like getting angry, but I felt it rising up. It just felt totally unjust, rude, and disrespectful. It shouldn't* *happen in the church. It shouldn't happen when you are about to lead worship. There should be kindness and gentleness. Where is the love and patience and kindness?*

There is a pain in unmet needs, in overload and burnout, and in feeling devalued. There is pain associated with ongoing or broken relationships as well as hurts inflicted by leaders and others. All these we will consider under relevant thematic headings, but we should also note that leaving can bring its own pain and for some leavers, regardless of whether they join another church or not, there can be a variety of deep hurts. The very common feelings of disappointment, abandonment or anger are sometimes accompanied by a type of discomfort which Aaron described as 'withdrawal.' The treatment he had found effective was going back to foundations rather than just finding another church to attend. In his case, this was closely examining the trustworthiness of the Bible as the 'Word of God:'

Aaron: *For me, I've unpicked the hard wiring in me because there is so much wrong with that thing called church. My wife suffered more, but it opened up many conversations. She has had her own withdrawal to go through. When I had the accident is when I started my research and I said on what basis is my faith? The only* *thing I can rely on is the word of God, so can I trust it? I wasn't interested at first in reading it but in finding out if it is the inspired word of God. My research led me to the conclusion that, from a logical perspective, we could stand on what it said.*

Needs Not Met

Although in the chats, it was not frequently expressed overtly, some leavers noted that while in church, their needs had not been met. We will consider the issue of personal and relational needs when we look at relationships, but it may be interesting to note here how Ben represents those who cite needs not met in terms of lacking the sort of engaging activities that would stimulate interest:

Ben: *I think that probably... I'm about a quarter of the church-going man I used to be back in the late 80s because I just can't find anything to attract me. I go along and keep in touch with spiritual things, and obviously, you have your own personal walk, but it wouldn't be difficult for me to drop out of church-going altogether and yet still call myself a Christian and still know I'm saved and not scared of death and so on... I'd like to be going to a thriving church that was taking my interest not just on Sunday morning but at least a couple of other times during the week and with men's prayer groups, 6 O'clock Wednesday morning sort of thing, or a supper, certainly a house group meeting weekly and getting close relationships with people, praying with them and being able to respond when there are crises in their lives.*

Agnes expressed the idea of needs not being met in a sort of resignation to the reality that church would not be able to meet her deepest personal needs:

Agnes: *But I think I've got to the point now where I'm not even looking to the church to meet my needs as I see them. I'm not looking to any institutional church to be able to meet my needs or meet my dreams or my heart's desire or whatever God's planted in me anymore. I've just kind of gone. Alright, that's not going to happen, forget it. I want to be able to go and worship God and I would like to be able to connect with people and that's basically all I want, which is, like a bit reduced...*

As we will see later, the capacity of churches to meet people's needs, including their deep personal and relational needs, seems related to a number of factors. These include their theology, their concept of purpose in reaching and ministering to various groups and the capabilities and behaviors of their leaders. It is also complicated by the obvious difficulties of human relationships in any type of organization. In extreme cases, the failure to meet needs has even been described as a type of abuse:

Jocelyn: *I had been to Upton Hope Church and the words I use to describe life there was spiritual abuse. Very good on the word and worship-wise, polished.*

Good when I started, but I had real concerns that people were sitting there with huge needs that were brushed under the carpet.

Overload and Burnout

The capacity of churches to overload willing volunteers as well as paid staff is widely recognized and was well represented in the chats. As with any organization relying heavily on volunteers, there is often a great benefit to those serving as well as to the organization. However, churches seem to suffer from their enterprise being regarded as a spiritual one which predisposes leaders and others to see volunteers as God's resources and the cause as being of greater worth than the well-being of its supporters. For some, this is experienced as a sort of toxic spiritualization. It has the power to depersonalize the service offered by individuals and characteristically overburdens 'willing workhorses' who can get to the point where they can't bear the strain anymore. It also seems to be coupled with poor communication, which means overburdened individuals feel that they are not being really listened to.

Kaylee: *It's not just no interest shown in us as people. In the light of the leadership we had and the commitment we showed—it was as though there was just an expectation that it would be more, but 'No!' One of the reasons why the church is so poor at looking after the people who are very resourceful is that they think God will provide. It's like missionaries who don't say* *thank you because it's God's money anyway! To us, it's a massive relief to get out. We just feel it's no skin off their nose because, well, [adopting a cynical tone expressed in 3rd person] 'God will provide. God always provides and we are in the Holy Spirit here. God's looking after us.'*

Another factor leading to increased stress is the lack of effective support and training for the various roles and jobs that need doing in church, whether this arises through a lack of systematic planning or, as in Evelyn's case, gaps created by other people leaving that are not filled effectively:

Evelyn: *I was also quite exhausted 'cause I was doing lots of stuff and not really being supported. Nahum had been doing my worship mentoring. When he left, I thought, I learned there's a lot more to it than just standing there and singing.*

Being Valued

If the overload is a problem for some, then others seem to have experienced almost the opposite—a feeling of not being useful or valued personally.

Declan: *I started to feel that I didn't have any value. The new leader wanted to do things himself. He took the website off me and ended up doing it himself. New people would come in and I was not needed anymore. Feeling valued can take different forms. There are people down at ULC that I really enjoyed being with and I felt valued, but a lot of them have gone. I don't feel as if they want anything out of me anymore.*

Jocelyn: *I kept asking the Lord to leave, but he said, 'No,' but eventually I got the house divided scripture, so I left. I went to let them know and they accepted it so easily I was obviously a dispensable member of the congregation.*

One shared experience is that of being 'dropped' from roles, responsibilities or areas of service, usually without participation in the decision and often with little communication as to the reason. When this happens, it conveys a lack of valuing a person and hints at programmes and activities as being more important than people, especially where they have previously been acknowledged as having skills and talents that the church can use:

Emilia: *I did a poster and some tracts to go with it. I went in and heard X (a leader) say he had done something and they'd spent a lot of money on it. They wanted his contribution but not mine. I was upset. I'd done all that work and they just steamrolled his idea out. I thought there was no point in saying anything to them. They've made up their minds.*

The perceived value of new people over those already in the church is noted by a few leavers as a cause for concern and, as we shall see later, this seems related to some churches' views about purpose and mission. There's certainly a common thread well expressed by Evelyn.

Evelyn: *There's no pastoring, no love for the people already there. There are always new people coming in but others leaving 'cause they are not being looked after.*

Theme 2: Relationships

Now I am giving you a new commandment: Love each other. Just as I have loved you should love each other. Your love for one another will prove to the world that you are my disciples.'

John 13:34-35 NLT

Love is patient and kind. Love is not jealous or boastful or proud or rude. It does not demand its own way. It is not irritable, and keeps no record of being wronged. It does not rejoice about injustice but rejoices whenever the truth wins out. Love never gives up, never loses faith, is always hopeful, and endures through every circumstance.'

1 Corinthians 13:4-7 NLT

Living out Love

The life, teaching and example of Jesus can surely leave us in no doubt about the primacy of love in Christian's faith. How sad it is then to realize that in the experience of many leavers, the church has sometimes been far from a loving experience. Like Avicii and Garrix they can leave church and instead find themselves 'Waiting for Love' elsewhere (1).

Love as Care, Concern or Contradiction

We saw in stark terms earlier on how a perceived lack of care had profoundly affected one leaver. To say *'They just don't care'* about anyone in a church, let alone the leaders, seems astonishing in the light of our usual expectations of church and Christians. But I know, through my own repeated experience and that of others, just how common this is felt and how it can be a significant factor in the decision to leave.

Is it actually true that church leaders and others in churches simply don't care? That seems counter-indicated by the overt focus of so much church activity on caring and helping in so many different ways and certainly the focus of one hundred and one sermons and verbal exhortations.

So what happened? How can an institution that talks up love so much and is filled with so many caring people end up creating this impression of so little personal care in so many cases? There is probably a clue in the word institution, and we will consider that later.

It is certainly not an unusual perception for leavers to feel that something about church has reduced the capacity for others to care for them even as much as their non-Christian friends and family. Let's be clear that we are not talking only about leaders or just a small group deliberately doing this to others. The experiences reported suggest that caring has been absent from leaders and 'followers' alike.

Morris: *When you go to church and they say, How are you? ...How many people actually want to know? Or is it a standard greeting? I can think of four or five people who, if I turn up on Sunday, say to me, 'Oh, how are you?' and then they are scoping out the next person they're going to see. They don't even wait for me to answer. And I think, 'You're not bothered. You don't really want to know how I am.' it just really annoys me. If you don't want to know how I am, just say, 'Hi. That's fine.'*

Is there something about the institutional church that creates what seems to be this great inconsistency or contradiction? Some leavers feel that it reflects the functional view of people as serving the institution, which makes them more like cogs in a machine rather than parts of one body. This seems indicated by experience. Agnes shared that the care seemed linked to roles or jobs in the church and a sense of being invisible without that.

Agnes: *I've noticed that when you're doing a job, it's almost like people notice you, but when you stop doing a job and you are just a member of the congregation,* *you become quite invisible. That's kind of my experience of church.*

Sometimes the capacity to provide and experience care and concern has something to do with the size of the church or group. It seems that smaller settings are more likely to provide environments perceived as caring as they facilitate more intimate human interactions than larger institutions.

Jayden: *Where I met God particularly is at Salem, but even more at the small house group. We pray together and discuss things. If I'm not there, I get a message to say, 'Where are you? We feel lost without you.' They know you are not around. I value that. It comes from concern, at least, from attempting to meet me as a human being.*

Does familiarity breed contempt? One idea commonly expressed by leavers was that while the church had demonstrated care and concern in the early days, that had not been evident as time passed and they had become established members or even leaders within the church. This is sometimes linked to the specific ministry of pastoral care within churches:

Kaylee: *The church is quite good at bringing people in, but it is not good at pastoring people. We were there for seven years, but there was zero interest in us and in our spiritual journey.*

In the face of increasing institutionalism, some leavers recognize the importance of not giving in to institutional pressure by assuming the institution will do the caring but, instead making it an aim at an individual level:

Julian: *You can get institutionalized in anything. I like to encourage people: for me; I value the informal stuff. I try to show that the church does care without even really noticing. I don't mind the occasional rebuff. I stay on the edges, but it is a task I can do. There are old St. Stephen's people who looked out for people. They might not be on the same wavelength, but they cared enough to try.*

Love as Family

Numerous writers with significant experience of founding and running churches recognise the huge difference that sometimes exists between the family love commanded by Jesus and the actual behaviour of Christians towards their brothers and sisters 'in Christ'. This is noted honestly by Terry Virgo (2) who founded a global movement of over 800 churches in more than sixty nations.

The common claim that church is family is seriously challenged by the experience of many leavers. Some note that the metaphor of the family is not a fitting one for church at all, especially when the message from leaders is that you are not really a member unless you fit in and comply with leaders or the prevailing culture. In that case, perhaps a more fitting metaphor is that of a train, as Morris suggested, where someone who doesn't fit in can get off at the next station.

Morris: *You don't say to your family, 'You don't fit in, off you go,' do you? Some families might, but not in an ideal family. I'd be interested to know what their definition of family is because the entire authenticity and the hypocrisy of the way ULC works hinges on what they're selling themselves as. I'm very aware of* *what their behavior is and how the church works from my perspective: it's a train. The passengers on the train can't get through to the train driver because there's a locked door. The train driver knows exactly where he's going, what speed he's going at and how he's going to get there. He's in charge...*

The family metaphor is not as simple as is often suggested. It is not usually taken to refer to parent/child hierarchies but to close human relationships. These are certainly far from perfect but are essentially loving and caring toward those within. There is growth within families as children mature and this can be a source of tension. In churches, however, there is often the sense of being let down by family members from whom much more was expected. This could be because of genuinely poor care, but it might also represent, as Peter Scazzero notes (3), a process of enlightenment and maturing by which we become more aware of the fallibility of others as well as ourselves and in which we lose the unrealistic expectation that the family of the church can be a place where no one lets us down and we are always well treated. The mantra, 'There is no perfect church,' may well reflect the truth that there is no perfect family.

Love as Friendship

If leavers sometimes note that churches fall short in living up to their promise of being family, then it is also noted by some that friendship can be an inconsistent aspect of church life. Significant friendships have been, for some, their introduction to church:

Nigel: *The very first thing was friendship. People got to know you, really nice people that we'd never met before. They were coming up and being quite welcoming and friendly, so it opened up a whole new friendship base.*

It seems in this respect, as in others, that the size and setting of the church can be an important factor:

Jayden: *The church I go to now, we are sat around a table, and we share scripture together. We share songs together. We share a bit like a group of friends in a house. I've been involved with larger congregations, but they leave me feeling a little bit cold.*

Once people have left a church, it is common for them to reflect on the depth of friendships that existed. Morris and Agnes noted this forcefully earlier as a surprising level of disinterest, but Declan seems to suggest that the loss of friendship is a predictable outcome of people joining other friendship circles or leaving in significant numbers:

Declan: *There are a lot of people who have walked out. They've gone out the back door, so you not only lose members of the church. You lose friends. You make friends at church, don't you? You might only see them in church contexts, but if they leave, they make friends elsewhere.*

Loving Speech and Actions

We saw earlier how some leavers had been hurt by others and we now consider some specific features that were mentioned as problematic.

In Kaylee's case, we see the impact of a range of behaviors that made her feel devalued despite the contributions she was making as a leader and on a personal hospitality level. The behaviors themselves don't seem extreme when compared with the sordid church scandals that make press headlines. But over time, they were part of a pattern of behavior that undermined her belonging:

Kaylee: *The people who came to our house and had meals again and again and in the morning at church would walk by me without even looking at me. I thought, what's going on here? I don't do this to be thanked, but surely church people should be exemplary with manners. Everything that has happened since leaving has been a confirmation of our decision. It's been a closed shop. I got teased regularly for my accent and my 'posh' voice. It was okay most of the time, but when I was tired, I felt I didn't belong.*

There is a fairly common notion, often supported in stereotypical fashion by the media that churches are judgemental. This was not widely expressed by leavers but had some support:

Ralph: *We all want to be seen as reasonable, but I think when I was a young man and as a Christian, I was a bit of a fundamentalist. I look at stuff the church comes out with and I don't know whether I believe that anymore. It feels like the Christian church is the last bastion of acceptable prejudice. It's okay to be prejudiced against gays and trans and druggies and so on. I have the feeling if Jesus came back now, he'd be at the front of a gay pride march. There's a guy who says, 'Love them all and let God sort them out,' the gay or the couple who are living together. I haven't walked in their shoes. I'd like to say I'd got it all sorted out but not so. The church as a whole body; I've become less comfortable with it. I'm not a fan of finger-pointing.*

The negative perception of churches and Christians was reported by one of our leavers as having been a barrier in coming to faith:

Garth: *That church down there. My granddad used to run it. That was a big part of it, but my dad left, and he was supposed to be a Christian. That side of the family had nothing to do with it. My view of it was kind of tainted. Oh, these Christians, they didn't want to have anything to do with me. I kind of had that view* *from 16 to 21 about my family and those Christians and saw them all the same way.*

If there is a tendency to judge, it seems that it is sometimes experienced by those within as well as outside the church. For Ruby, a series of conversations caused her to feel hindered from participation by being judged as unsuitable for a leading role because of her family situation:

Ruby: *A leader said, 'Ruby, we need people up there whose lives aren't a mess. This is why, if people are in the worship team, they have to be this and that.' I said, 'Honey, I'm too long in the tooth to hear this conversation. If you want perfect, you'll have no one leading and no one in worship and no one doing nothing, so don't even go there.'*

In Jocelyn's case, the judgment was felt as a sort of public knowledge about her personal life:

Jocelyn: *I felt very judged because everybody was looking in on the scenario and they all had their ideas about what they thought. That became quite public. For me, I kind of stepped back.*

Sometimes the behaviors identified in both speech and action can be very destructive of loving relationships and can lead to catastrophic relationship breakdowns:

Patricia: *I know that at the time when we did actually leave ULC, one of the reasons was that we actually saw something happening between people that did quite quickly snowball and it was like a bomb going off in there. We weren't seeing the right thing going on. It affected a lot of people and, from the leaders' view, because they had to handle that, it must have been really difficult.*

A major part of such breakdowns is when we take offense at what others say or do. The damaging effect of taking offense cannot be overestimated in the life of any church. It is a denial of the forgiveness that is at the heart of the Christian's faith and arguably one of the most destructive forces ruining relationships.

Patricia: *It's about relationships as well, but I suppose that's where we all need to grow up in Christ and not be offended.*

We might all agree that Christians should be the first to apologize and the last to take offense, but working this out in practical terms can prove difficult as demonstrated by two very different, and possibly contradictory, approaches as Ruby mentioned them:

Ruby: *A leader gave a sermon saying that he used to say that people who hurt people should have to apologize. Now he believes that as older mature Christians, we should forgive and not seek an apology* *and we should move on and walk in love. (But I believe) If you've hurt someone, you've got to have that meeting, apologize, move on and build bridges for both your sake. You know, it's called learning. That's what I believe.*

Communication on Leaving

It is very common for poor communication to be cited as a factor during the leaving process and for this to be taken as evidence of the weakness of a church in demonstrating love:

Ruby: *So far, the only person that's contacted me is A. Well, B has also reached out, but nobody from the leadership and no one else from church—and they know all the problems. They didn't even text me. I'd expected X (the leader) to text both of us.*

Nathan suffered a similar absence of communication when he no longer attended, but he noted that such behaviors are further evidence that churches are part of a dysfunctional worldly system.

Nathan: *Nobody called me to find out if I'd left or why. It just emphasizes the fact that the system isn't working. That's what it is, a system. It's not the true church of Christ, is it? I left another church and I'd not been in a church till I came to Upton. This coming to a church in Upton emphasized that I was right before. I had left the system.*

Where there was an acknowledgment of communications from a church after the point of leaving, our leavers rarely reported it as a positive experience. Scarlett noted the tendency for ongoing communication to feel as if it has only the intention of drawing leavers back into the church:

Scarlett: *There's a feeling of being hounded. There was one church where I did feel a little bit like that. I almost had to hide from people: the leader and his wife, because they would basically be saying, 'We really miss you, we really want you to come back.' It wasn't about, 'Where are you now?'*

It is interesting to note, however, that she challenges very rigorously the perception that leavers are always the victims of poor communication:

Scarlett: *Some manipulative people just want attention. You could run around after them and completely wear yourself out. For a while, in my cross-state, I wanted to sit upstairs and did not want people to communicate with me. I've often been thinking about why people sit upstairs and drift in and drift out. I was happy to turn up late so I could sneak in and then go. I never understood people who did that, but I do now. It's like contacting people, texting them, are you hounding them? If you do it only once or twice, people say you don't care because you never contacted me. Some people will point-blank lie about not being contacted to fuel their isolation.*

While many leavers pointed out aspects of poor leadership communication, it was recognized by some that the responsibility to communicate well lies with everyone. Those who, for example, are overworked in the church need to signal the truth to leaders even if they feel they are letting the side down:

Agnes: *I realize now that what I could have done, and what I would do now, is go and say, 'I've got too much on my plate, too much responsibility, and I need you to lighten my load.'*

Theme 3: Leadership

Jesus called them together and said, "You know that the rulers in this world lord it over their people, and officials flaunt their authority over those under them. But among you it will be different. Whoever wants to be a leader among you must be your servant, and whoever wants to be first among you must become your slave...".

Matthew 20:25-27

Dear brothers and sisters, honour those who are your leaders in the Lord's work. They work hard among you and give you spiritual guidance. Show them great respect and wholehearted love because of their work. And live peacefully with each other.

1 Thessalonians 5:12-13

The model of servant leadership promoted by Jesus himself is in sharp contrast to the usual human forms of leadership and authority. This is also evident in many New Testament metaphors for the Church, not least the 'priesthood of all believers' (1 Peter 2:9) and the various references to the Body of Christ (such as 1

Corinthians 12:12 – 31), under Christ the head (Colossians 1:18). It is sometimes pointed out that biblical leadership is one function or calling among many and that where there is a biblical list of functions or ministries, leadership is either not specifically included or is near the bottom of the list (as in the fivefold ministry 'gifts' of Ephesians 4:11 and the 'parts of the body' in 1 Corinthians 12:28).

Despite this revolutionary approach, most churches and denominations continue to rely on hierarchical or institutional 'top-down' leadership. The 'head' of the body is said to be Christ, but it is clear that even in 'free churches' where the senior leaders are not called 'priests' or 'vicars' they are still given titles such as 'pastor' to indicate their position as distinct from, and sometimes above, their fellow believers rather than to simply identify a particular gift or ministry. This inevitably indicates the persistence of a priestly or clerical caste and was clearly identified as long ago as 1934 by Watchman Nee, who drew a helpful distinction for us, particularly between the pastoral gift and the pastoral system.

In addition to the overt or implied intermediary role, there are, no doubt, many consequences of priestly clericalism within churches. Aaron notes how professionalizing leadership creates a tendency to passivity within the church body:

Aaron: *There's a gulf between laity and clergy... They have taken on the man-made interpretation of the word. As soon as you pay someone, it all changes. I've seen this in Germany. A really good man in the congregation took up a pastor's role unpaid. It was good, but then we paid him and he became a professional. The central problem is that it's all man-made leadership. It's not God-ordained. The consequence is that we end up with church goers who become passive.*

Another consequence of identifying leadership in this very human way is the tendency to expect them to be able to solve all the problems and to take on not just roles for which they have been gifted but leadership for all the functions of church life. In our chats, some leavers indicated particular appreciation for the difficult work of those in leadership:

Patricia: *From their perspective, trying to run a church, it must be one of the hardest jobs in the world because you've got all these different people that you're supposedly looking after and shepherding and teaching and all the problems associated with it. It must be* *extremely difficult. You can never please all the people all the time and you can never have the perfect church.*

Leadership Competence and Behaviours

Leavers sometimes express concern about the competence of church leaders to do things in a safe way when they try to meet the needs of very vulnerable people:

Declan: *They've taken on stuff they are not qualified for. Looking after homeless seemed very sensible, but dealing with social issues and mental health—they are not qualified. I'm worried it's going to bite. It's going to come back and bite. They are dealing with some people who are deeply scarred. This is an area for experts. They can do damage to people, serious damage.*

There is sometimes the perception of assumed expertise that can cause leaders to lose sight of how people are being affected within the church:

Ben: *People who go there tell us the leadership lives in cloud cuckoo land even though they are going around the world talking about the communities. It's caused a complete split in the church. Almost all the people we knew when we were going there have left. In some cases, they have left and gone to different parts of the country, or they've gone to other churches. In some cases, they've just dropped out altogether.*

There is a common perception among leavers that leaders don't or can't listen well. Scazzero emphasizes the importance of listening to God and to others as a means of establishing and maintaining deep connections based on love and which, historically, have often been sacrificed to religious activity by church leaders (5).

Not listening has an impact on the leaders' capacity to understand matters from the perspective of others:

Kaylee: *They have no understanding because they have not been listening. There is no understanding whatsoever of what you have been at great pains to point out.*

This weakness in the ability to listen effectively can have serious impacts, especially in situations where individuals have made themselves vulnerable in sharing with the leaders concerned:

Agnes: *I had a one to one with a leader some years ago. To say what I really feel, there has to be quite a lot of trust there. So I made this appointment and I went and I was really honest about how I was feeling. It would have gone so much better if that leader had said, 'I'm really sorry, but although we've booked this time to talk, I've now found that I've got another job that I've got to attend to, so it's going to have to be ten minutes.' What actually happened was that they looked out of the window or at the clock. They sat just there and looked thoroughly disengaged, so by the time I'd finished. I felt like I'd just made myself completely vulnerable. That* *changed my approach to church. I go in, I shut my eyes, I worship, and I talk to God, but I'm not talking to anyone else and then I go home.*

Some leavers feel that they have been treated badly by leaders but that the communication needed to restore relationships is too difficult to achieve:

Jocelyn: *Can you understand how hard it would be for me to go to them and say anything? I have felt like I need to have a conversation with them and say, 'I do forgive you.' I would need to say to them that I felt this was something that has been between us.*

Much of what we've noted above assumes a sort of united approach within leadership, but that may not be the case:

Josh: *I believe there's disunity at the center. One of the leaders came around a while back and started asking a whole lot of questions. He asked about worship on Sunday. He asked, 'Have you thought of leaving the church?' I said yes and he wasn't surprised. Other people have noted that there is friction. Maybe there's stuff going on that means leadership is just not on the same page.*

Sometimes lack of clear leadership communication creates insecurity or embarrassment:

Scarlett: *There are changes that occur that the church needs to know. For example that Y (a youth* *worker) has done youth work for so many years but has stepped down recently. She was given some flowers, but it should be acknowledged that that's what happened. When I stepped down from being ladies' leader, I had to keep saying to people, 'No, I'm not the ladies' leader anymore.' There's a public thing of being told who we are and that's happening, but then when that changes, there's no communication. Then you are in awkward situations where people either think you are just being really lazy or don't care. It's not your place to do that, but if you don't tell them that yourself, no one tells them.*

The influence of a leader's spouse was noted by a couple of leavers. While the role is often seen as crucial to the success of leadership, it can also present challenges:

Kaylee: *It doesn't help in the church that the leader's wife is so conflicted. She is a very divisive force in the church.*

Ruby: *The leader's spouse hasn't spoken to me properly in a year and a half and what interactions we have had were not productive, so I've got to step down. I can't be honest with my leadership if I'm in the doghouse. If it was anybody else, I would have said, 'Why are you being so patronizing and why are you being so angry with me?'*

Decision-Making

Declan's focus on decision-making had indicated a 'missing accountability of the leadership to the membership,' and leavers frequently point to autocratic decision-making in churches.

Ben: *I think in some churches, the leaders are autocratic. They want the people to do what they want and aren't prepared to do the sort of things that members of the congregation would like to do.*

Emilia: *More and more people are unhappy and more will leave, but the leaders are going on their course. This is what they've decided to do.*

An important aspect of leadership decision-making is identifying who gets consulted before a decision is made:

Nigel: *You could say it's petty if it's solely down to decision-making processes that they make, the way they decide to make decisions: whether to involve the bigger congregation in decision making, out of basic respect for the people that are coming to your church. In my mind, everybody was just totally ignored on that particular occasion about making a choice about doing something with the children's work. A lot of experienced Christians on the periphery of leadership circles were not consulted in any way or not asked what their opinions were. You felt like, because it's a young church* *as well, that there are stacks of experience there on the outside that you're not tapping into.*

Josh: *I reflected on the way things were being done, like a particular outreach program, when that got pulled, having been involved at an early stage in the kitchen work. I took it on and then it all just got withdrawn without any consultation. I saw through this a lack of engagement with the people who were actually making it work. Is there no consultation? They just guillotined it.*

Key to the process of decision-making and consultation that marks many churches out as being different to other institutions is a widely shared perception that it is God who leads the decision-making process. Most church leaders would agree with that, but they also often believe that it is to church leaders that God makes his will known. If that is unlike other institutions, then what seems very similar is the tendency to self-promotion and controlling others. In his insightful reflections on Christian leadership, Henri Nouwen recognises the persistent tendency throughout the history of the church for people to desire leadership, power and control rather than follow the example and teaching of Jesus (6)

In some churches, the leaders quote the mantra that 'church is not a democracy' along with the view of leaders as the ones who hear from God as their rationale for limited consultation. This is rarely overtly stated (I've checked the churches' websites) but is a factor noted by some leavers:

Jocelyn: *The leadership needs to be open to the fact that if they've not heard it quite right and lots of people are feeling similarly, then it might be useful to them to take on board what is said and think, well, maybe we've only heard part of it and we need to tweak it and listen to what is being said and actually, 'yeah, we did get a bit of it wrong.'*

Agnes: *it's an interesting idea that if you've got a bunch of leaders who believe that they've got a hotline and that they don't need to justify anything or even explain anything, but then you've got a congregation who have got the same hotline, theoretically, that you are a collective. But if you don't all listen to each other, then you are not a collective.*

Several church settings actively promote the right of leaders to make decisions without consultation, even where the subsequent changes have significant impacts on attendees' children and their experience of church. In Patricia's case, this seems to have included even a presumed right to talk to the children without parental involvement:

Patricia: *My feeling is definitely negative because of the way it was handled by the leadership. They didn't support us with moving and were telling us that what we were doing was detrimental to our children and that it brought disunity because that was voiced to them. Probably one of the most difficult things was the criticism over what we were doing to our children, completely ignoring the fact that the Lord gave us stewardship over our children.*

In Scarlett's case, her children were adversely affected by changes to the church's organization of children's and youth work. This led to the children disconnecting from church. As parents, she and George wanted their children to be fully involved in making decisions that affected the whole family. A similar approach to involvement in decision-making on the part of church leaders would involve meaningful consultation with those most likely to be affected. In this case, that could have been the children and parents themselves:

Scarlett: *There was a change to the way youth work was structured that just wrecked it for the girls. What happened on Friday changed completely. Sunday changed completely. We had two children that didn't* *want to go to church. We tried just the evening. One would go to that, the other hated it. We needed to just go once because it was the only time we had as a family. That also came at the same time. That highlighted that wherever we are, we are a family. We are not autocratic and dictate to them. We as a family need to discuss it. So there's been a disconnect for them too.*

Sometimes the sheer speed of leaders' decisions takes people by surprise:

Emilia: *Philip came back from (another region in the UK) and they decided very quickly to join up with an outreach program. The logo, the café was going to be changed, all very, very quickly. I presume it was Philip and Jacob and a few others. It's much easier to go ahead with a few people. I think Philip's personality is, 'Bang, bang, get on with it!'*

Leavers note a very common link between autocratic decision-making and poor communication:

Nigel: *It was down to decisions made which affected us as parents and which affected our children and a lack of communication. Things were just done (snaps fingers) like that, and you think, hang on, that shouldn't have been done that way. Surely we should have had some communication before. Just basic stuff.*

George: *There was a period of frustration and being sidelined. If you were happy in a place you were serving, you wouldn't want to leave, would you? If you were content where you are and fully connected. For me personally, what really narked me was being taken off the rota. They rang me up and said we want our best to lead services, so we're taking you off the rota. The decision... and the way it was bluntly put—almost like justifying it by talking about taking other people off rotas: it was a decision made and done.*

Values, Vision and Mission

Like many other organizations, churches are familiar with concepts of values, vision, purpose, mission, purpose, goals and so on. These are deeply meaningful concepts that, unfortunately, have lost some of their power due to overuse and misunderstanding. However, it is only against some understanding of the purpose of an action or program that it is possible to gauge success. It is also primarily by considering behaviors, actions and what is measured that we can discern what are the genuine values of a church, regardless of what the statements say.

Some churches are unclear about why they exist or there are differences between leaders or leaders and attendees in working this out. Some leavers express this as a type of disunity.

Josh: *In organizations, you have a clear focus on the goals. People are in agreement with the purpose of the organization. I imagine that a failing of churches is that there is not that collective agreement about the key goals of where the church is heading. The leaders at the church are not on the same page and it was obvious that there was no discussion at the leadership level—*

such disunity. When people are not aligned—I've seen mission statements, but they are not focused.

Other churches have clear statements of vision and mission, but actual practices, behaviors and actions of leaders themselves don't seem to line up with them and frequently indicate an agenda to establish a sort of independent little kingdom:

Patricia: *Leaders turning against you as new believers are always going to be a hard one to digest, but I think, for me, often what the trouble is in the church is that we lose the vision that we are building together, so we fall into the idea that your way is the right way, and you start building your own little empires.*

Most churches incorporate aspects of love, care and concern in their statements of values, vision and mission, but, as we noted earlier, that is not consistently experienced and it seems few churches attempt to gauge how well they are doing in love, care and concern. One of the few ways leaders would be able to do that is to diligently ask and listen. We noted earlier that this is often seen as a weakness in churches and it sometimes means that leaders pursue their own vision without drawing the whole church along with them:

Ben: *you need to be careful where your vision is taking you. If you're in an established church, common sense and decency would suggest you do it slowly and take people along with you. I think it's a problem with older people. I realize that young people are important, but I think what's happening is that old people are dropping off for different reasons. They are disenchanted with noise, particularly from music and children. They hate everything traditional being messed about with.*

In some cases, the values and vision of the leaders can be promoted, not just in ignorance but in deliberate disregard of attendees. Kaylee found this to be the case where she noted that despite repeated expressions of concern about the volume of the music, the leadership did not respond sensitively:

Kaylee: *...Noise, cacophonous noise in disregard of the congregation.*

An emphasis on 'outreach' to the detriment of pastoral care is frequently cited as a basis for disquiet. This seems commonly linked to churches' perceptions of their mission or purpose. The sense that churches are good at reaching out to new people but not great at disciplining, engaging or nurturing those already within has been noted by many:

Jocelyn: *For me, I feel like there's a lot of effort put in at the front door and not much at the back door. It's really sad.*

Church leaders sometimes refer to the great commission and other scriptures to promote an overt outreach emphasis backed up by popular sayings such as, *'The church is the only society that exists for the benefit of its non-members'* (William Temple). This seems appropriate until we consider how it can be used to support the notion that God is interested in new believers rather than those already in the church and the greater tolerance that churches can seem to have for new folk:

Ralph: *Sometimes, there are aspects of church that one becomes disenchanted with. Adrian Plass wrote about trying to win people for Christ and putting up with all sorts of things, but once they are in, they are expected to conform to the letter. It's like you've been here long enough and you should know better.*

A similar difference in approach influences the behavior of church leaders toward long-standing members and attendees who sometimes feel less worthy of care and attention than those outside the church. The vast numbers of people who have left churches without overt expressions of concern and dedicated attempts to retain or encourage communication suggest that they are seen as expendable or even as impediments to the mission of the church. There is sometimes the feeling that people who have been in church for a while, and especially those who have demonstrated leadership capacities themselves, should be 'fixed' or at least fully supportive of the church's mission and activities and that ongoing pastoral care is almost a distraction from the outreach mission:

Morris: *The brokenness they respond to, almost what I would call corporate brokenness, the brokenness that is almost easier to say, 'Hey, look at what we're doing.' The brokenness of people actually in the church just seems to be smoothed over. It's just kind of, 'Oh, we're giving some advice. If you don't listen to it, we're not going to talk to you again. If you don't listen to it, then you're not listening to God, so we're not going to engage with you again.' So the brokenness of the people who are already there just seems to not be even part of the way they think anymore. It's all got to be what we're doing and what we're seen to be doing.*

Declan: *We have heard, you have, I have, heard of instances where people have been treated badly by leadership, by a member of the leadership. You think, well, this isn't right, either being treated badly or ignored—people with problems. They open the doors for* *homeless, but people already in the church who have got problems and maybe are looking for help can get ignored.*

That does seem to be the point. I mean, you're not growing. You're just treading water. You bring new people in, but others are leaving by the back door.

Quality of Teaching

A minority of leavers expressed great appreciation for the teaching they had received. In Ben's case, this had fuelled his ability to make a stand for his faith and pass on his learning within a secular context. In this sense, he felt that the leader had met his responsibility to 'equip the saints for ministry':

Ben: *The church helped me incredibly when I first moved down here. I'd only been a Christian four years and I was determined at my first assembly to nail my colors to the mast and let them know I was a Christian, the church gave me the strength to do that because I felt totally fed. Often listening to one of the leader's sermons, I would get my assemblies for the whole week. I'd be inspired in that way and very often, there were several things he had said that I could just hang an assembly onto. All the staff knew I was a Christian and accepted that. They viewed me as totally honest: in a sense, church had fed that. Whether that's just my specific situation or whether every single person who is in the workplace needs that support—I would have thought they probably do.*

Other leavers, however, shared their view that there was something lacking in the teaching they had heard in church. Jocelyn expressed this as inadequate spiritual food and a variable standard over time:

Jocelyn: *There's not a huge amount of spiritual food in the teaching. I didn't think it was too bad when they were all saying it was really bad, but now it's even worse.*

Kaylee expressed her concerns in terms of the depth of teaching and hints that it is sometimes shallow because it reflects the limited experience of some leaders delivering it:

Kaylee: *There were quite a few times when it was embarrassingly shallow. People had been asked to talk, but there were no nuggets—just increasingly superficial. You would expect the senior leader to do the feeding. I guess what we are looking for is battle-scarred wisdom. That sort of depth.*

Issues around teaching sometimes seem to overlap in people's thinking. The depth of teaching is reflected by Nigel when he refers to 'good solid teaching,' but it also seems linked to the perception of good and bad doctrine. It is clear that in his case, the issue of teaching was a significant factor in his decision to leave a particular church:

Nigel: *The primary thing to move on from somewhere as we did was that the teaching wasn't as we perceived it to be. And then you start listening to* *established preachers that some would recommend you to listen to for good solid teaching and you are opened up even more to what actually should be being taught, or what you think should be being taught. That seems to make more sense and because you don't generally get that within the Sunday morning service at that point, you think, well, maybe we should move on and so it's like you're searching for a level of teaching that you think you should be getting and if it's not there you feel compelled to move on.*

We are often reminded that we live in a consumer society and those who warn us about treating church with the consumers' mindset are liable to point out that it is evidenced in the way we are able to pick and choose the type of teaching we value. This may make it easier to evaluate teaching in the local church as lacking in comparison to teaching that can be found elsewhere:

Emilia: *I get a lot of my teaching from other sources rather than the church, where it's all very basic teaching aimed at new Christians. I'm very concerned about the lack of being really true to the word. I think there's a lack of teaching on important issues. I get all my teaching from Derek Prince, David Pawson and so on. They are very true to the word and very clear.*

Prayer

A few leavers expressed their views about prayer in church. For the most part, this was not positive, but it was encouraging to hear Yuna talking about the value of 'ground-breaking prayer' that had been so helpful to her:

Yuna: *...What I experienced on Sunday is what being a Christian is about—personal growth, breaking those chains of addiction and depression. That is everything to me. If I didn't have ground-breaking prayer every now and then, it would be pointless for me.*

The more commonly expressed view by leavers who commented on prayer was that there wasn't enough of it in their most recent church or that there had been a decline in leadership commitment to prayer:

Declan: *That's another problem in the church. There's no prayer, no intercession—maybe a short one for the speaker, but apart from that, it's pretty rare. There is little solid prayer in the church. In the (another denomination) church, there's quite a lot of prayer. At New Life, there was much prayer and individual prayer during the meeting. There was time set aside for that. It is missing at ULC.*

Jocelyn: *So, prayer meetings. Don't get me started on that one. There aren't any, are there? When we had* *them, I went to them. I went to the early morning ones. Those are the things I would be at.*

Emilia: *We used to have prayer meetings. Then they didn't happen. I said this to the leader. I gleaned from him that it was his family time and he wasn't prepared to give it up. He didn't have the desire, he wasn't prepared to do that. I've spoken to him several times about that, you know, would it be possible to have that prayer and worship time? The last time we had prayer meetings, we prayed at 6 o'clock in the morning. There were no other leaders there. The feedback was that a lot of them are too busy or live far away.*

Nathan noted a qualitative issue about prayer when he expressed his strong reaction to the church not praying for believers elsewhere who had recently suffered severe persecution or hardship:

Nathan: *It's atrocious. Those are our brothers. To not even pray for them. It's shocking.*

Music and 'Worship'

There is a tendency in many churches to regard the musical or sung element of service as the 'worship' component of that service. This was not commonly noted as an issue by leavers, but Aaron had a perspective that it was actually a very significant psychological element in the errors that have been adopted within church thinking and practice:

Aaron: *Worship is so much deeper than just a few songs. We always need to backtrack and look to the source. Why are we doing these things? We've copied the world. Our churches are run like businesses. They are seeker friendly. Worship is the center-ground in that. Perhaps all of us need to distance ourselves so we can get back to our real roots. If you take the music out of these churches, what's left? Often an emotional moment. It's not a case of rearranging furniture, it's deep. It's perfect from Satan's point of view. Trance-like states lead to altered consciousness. Some people have commented on Christian services and recognized this. Once in a trance-like state, people become very susceptible to suggestions. When I came out of that church denomination, it happened while I was leading worship on the piano. I just came to a realization that I needed to stop. I had quite enjoyed the effect that I had on others I knew. I didn't mean to manipulate others:*

some quiet moments, creating an atmosphere. I believe now that the Lord was asking me to put it down.

Along similar lines is the view that it is possible to seduce people into experiencing what they mistake as a Holy Spirit experience because music can be so powerful at moving the soul. Some leavers indicate this is revealed in the vacuousness, confusion or plain error of the lyrics.

Declan: *What's happened is that the music has become all. It's the music that's important. It's also very loud and the stuff that is sung is catchy and good music, good riffs and things, but when you analyze the words, you find out what you are really singing. A lot of it is garbage. What does it mean to sing 'you unravel me with a melody?' What the heck does that mean? It's like the Beatles: a lot of their later stuff, the words are garbage, but the melodies are terrific. I think if you get the right music, you can sing absolute garbage and it still sounds good. It seems to me that's what is happening to church music.*

The most commonly expressed concern about music was the excessive volume. However, comments about this related to just one of the churches involved.

Kaylee: *That friend Chloe brought said she was going to have to bring her headphones next time and she was told off: that you must never criticize the* *worship leader. That person made a valid comment that it was too loud!*

Nathan: *For some reason, the music started to get so loud that my wife, who is disabled, couldn't stand it. I had a word with the leader asking, 'Is it possible that you could turn the music down?' He said, 'We can't do that. It's part of who we are as a church.'*

If there's a perception that loud music is necessary to reach out to young people, at least one leaver does not regard it as a successful strategy in this locality.

Emilia: *I've heard that the only way to reach young people is to have loud music. The day I did go, they had some young people, and they really didn't like it and they thought they were too old for it.*

Theme 4: The Nature of Church

Let us not neglect our meeting together, as some people do, but encourage one another, especially now that the day of his return is drawing near.

Hebrews 10:25

Christ is also the head of the Church, which is his body...

Colossians 1:18a

You are living stones that God is building into his spiritual temple. What's more, you are his holy priests... you are a chosen people, you are royal priests, a holy nation, God's very own possession.

1 Peter 1:9a

Institutionalism and What Leavers Think of as Church

All the churches known to history are quasi-political structures, institutions in a legal sense. In this legalistic, semi-political nature of the churches, their character as institutions appears most prominently and it is precisely this factor which distinguishes them most sharply from the Ecclesia of the New Testament and divides them from it by an impassable gulf.

Emil Brunner, 1952 *(7)*

There are a number of writers who see little or no connection between visible churches and the true Church. The most radical of these, like Charles Newbold, see churches as the *'harlot church system'* from which all true believers should come out. *(8)* Less radically, Frank Viola and George Barna see churches as having strayed historically in huge measure from the *ekklesia* of the New Testament. They urge a return from 'pagan Christianity' to an 'organic,' non- or less-institutional church. *(9)* Closer to the traditions with which we have become familiar are those like Francis Chan who emphasize that 'we are church' and are encouraging us all to be church in a very different way without abandoning the institutional churches wholesale. In his book, *'Letters to the Church'* (10), Chan advocates strongly for the unity of *'being'* church together as foundational for missiological success.

There is undoubtedly a pressing question about how well the church represents Jesus himself. Many see the two as synonymous and leave *'disappointed with Jesus'* (11) due to their church experience. Even well-known Christians like Bear Grylls often articulate their perceived misidentification of church and institutional religion with true faith in Jesus Christ. Grylls addresses this issue with powerful personal conviction in his 2021 autobiography *'Never Give Up'* (12).

Many people in the world nowadays identify the church as a seriously flawed religious institution and individual churches as local religious clubs for hypocrites or the feeble-minded. Inside churches there are millions desperate for change, especially if that can be, as Chan advocates, a move back to first principles. Or is it too late? Have institutional churches become so corrupt, so pagan, so out-of-date, so worldly or so irrelevant that the only way is out?

In his brilliantly researched book, *'The Invisible Church: Learning from the experience of churchless Christians'* (13), Steve Aisthorpe offers the optimistic conclusion that the Church is going through one of its major transitions and that a new Church is emerging. He encourages us to be hopeful about future expressions of corporate Christianity and not to grieve too much the demise of the institutions of churches and even the concept of the 'local church' that for so long has represented the operational outworking of the true Church.

In his follow-up work, *'Rewilding the Church'* (14), Aisthorpe issues a challenging call to reconsider the very nature of the Church in contrast to institutional Christianity and to let it be *rewilded*. This rewilding is a clarion call to allow the Holy Spirit to radically transform the Church rather than to vainly persist in supporting existing structures. It is not, however, a prompt to simply leave churches:

> *The attempted resuscitation of dying congregations is a tragic diversion and not to be confused with the resurrection of the Church. The former is often the preoccupation of the institutional centre; the latter tends to happen on the fringe.*
> *The rewilding of the Church draws on the resurrection power at its heart through innovation, asking new questions and going back to foundational considerations, refocusing on following Jesus and loving neighbours and being open-minded about what emerges.*

Steve Aisthorpe, 2020 *(15)*

A number of leavers expressed opinions within this range of responses giving credence to Brunner's (1952) view of the *'impassable gulf'* between the institutional churches to which we have become accustomed and the original Church *(ekklesia)* of the New Testament. Nowhere is this more evident than in the widespread confusion caused by the very word 'church.'

Aaron: *We should cut it (the word church) adrift. I don't think it's just terminology. It's in our very understanding of the word. You end up saying you can't GO to church because church is not a place. I brought my children up to 'go to church' and now they look at me. They go to church, but mum and dad don't go to church. They are hardwired to think that way.*

This key component of institutional 'churchianity' is the priority given to buildings which has created the impression in the world at large that church is a place to 'go to.' Several leavers rejected the 'go to a building' perspective:

Nathan: *People are part of the church. It doesn't matter where we meet. They meet in what we call church buildings, but that's not church, really. I still have fellowship with a number of Christians but not in them.*

In his book, *'The Spirit Filled Church: Finding your place in God's purpose'* (16), Terry Virgo offers a helpful emphasis on the priority of fellowship rather than just attendance together at a building, but he expresses great concern about those who are not committed to a local group of believers.

Virgo's position is helpfully based on a clear perception of the church as a group of people—the *ekklesia* of a *'local assembly'* and not as simply attendance at a building. His exhortations help to articulate greater meaning to the well-known expression, 'DON'T JUST GO TO CHURCH – BE THE CHURCH'. It may be worth suggesting here that, when thinking about church attendance, it is as inaccurate to equate attendance *'at church'* with commitment to Christian fellowship as it is to equate non-attendance with a lack of commitment *per se*.

Declan: *I've been studying more and more about the kingdom and where my faith should be with the Lord. I've realized that there is much more involved in being a Christian, It's not just a case of turning up.*

Given the historical experience of Christians all over the world and through two millennia, along with the natural behaviors of human beings in social settings, there is a common view that institutionalism is an inevitable process:

Agnes: *Maybe in a really organized corporate church of any size, once you start putting on coffee mornings, and outreach, and men's group, prayer group and toddlers' group, youth group and evening services, it* *becomes more about the agenda, the practical timetable.*

Leavers frequently mention the dangers of institutionalism in church, although this rarely takes quite the radical turn expressed by those who agree with Viola's assessment of common church practices and structures as expressions of 'Pagan Christianity' as noted above. Nathan made a telling reference to what he sees as the Biblical pattern for structuring meetings in a way that promotes leadership by the Holy Spirit and avoids institutional structures. His comment reflects Viola's promotion of the Biblical pattern for church meetings and is an obvious reference to 1 Corinthians 14:26-33:

Nathan: *There is not an obvious structure. The Holy Spirit gives gifts. Coming out of the organization doesn't disable the Holy Spirit. When you meet together, one will have a psalm, one will have a tongue. That's where the structure is—not in leadership.*

The commitment to fellowship outside of churches was not as common a theme as I had expected. This may be because most leavers contributing had joined other churches, or it could perhaps evidence the 'hold' of the institutional church as noted earlier. Certainly, I did not chat with as many leavers for whom this was a significant experience as I had expected.

Leaving aside the matter of fellowship, for some leavers, there's a clear distinction between any institutionalism and the personal faith that transcends institutions:

Julian: *Over and above the institutional manifestations, there is the quiet personal response to things and one's own relationship with God whether you are in or out of any particular institution.*

Money

Some leavers expressed concerns specifically over money. This might be how church money was being spent or questions raised by the apparent wealth of leaders in churches where attendees are funding church work and salaries:

Kaylee: *We tried not to see what we were seeing. You can't help noticing, though, when the person you have just funded rocks up in a brand-new expensive make of car. Whatever the reasons, it is just unwise in that type of church. And then the leader's car is also parked next to it, knowing that he just brought a brand-new house, built a house with everything in it— everything brand new, and then you question where is your money going?*

A few leavers indicated a link between financial decisions in the church and some notional accountability to those who provide the funds. Another aspect of this is the feeling that financial support can be linked to broader commitment or support:

Declan: (Sarcastically) *Oh, the leaders have made a decision, but they don't seem to have asked anybody else, like the people who pay their wages.*

God's Will, Leading and Involvement

Several leavers expressed views about the subject of churches, leaders and individuals being led by God. There's clearly a shared view that church processes and decisions don't always reflect God's leading:

Emilia: *A lot of them (leaders) are young men. They are enthusiastic. They believe that they are doing the right thing. My question is that it's not necessarily doing the right thing but doing what pleases God and doing specifically what the Holy Spirit is calling you to do. That can be very different.*

Some leavers claim to have been led by God to leave a specific church or to give up attendance there:

Emilia: *I also get a lot of my main fellowship, not from the church. I have a prayer triplet every week and the prayer for the town. Obviously, nobody wants to leave somewhere you've been part of and where you've invested right from the beginning. It's quite sad, the thought I might leave, but I find in my life—you often have to take the more lonely road and go with what God's saying.*

Nathan: *I went before the lord when my wife could not even leave the home she was in. I asked the Lord if he wanted me in the church. He said don't even cross the threshold, so I haven't since:*

Patricia: *The last time we left, it was very much the Lord. Yes, there were things that we'd been struggling with and decisions that had been made that we felt had changed something and our hearts just weren't there anymore...*

Well, He prepared us and it was time to move. I think it was a different path as well. There may have been things that we were uncomfortable with, but we probably would have made peace with that in some way if the Lord had wanted us to stay, but it was like we were picked up and put down again.

We considered earlier the matter of perceived poor leadership communication and in Agnes' case, this was seen as detrimental to her God-given calling and the use of her gifts of service which she felt church leaders didn't recognize. In this sense, she felt that she had left being actively involved before actually leaving:

Agnes: *I feel like, as a Christian, I've been on that journey. I've wholeheartedly prayed, and listened to God, 'What have you deposited? What have you given me? Right, that's what you want me to do about it.' I've gone to leadership, put it out there, talked and... nothing. So I don't actually use my gifting now.*

Such experiences may often be linked to people feeling the need to leave, but Scarlett noted the importance of waiting on God's lead rather than hastily misinterpreting his will by allowing difficult circumstances to cloud vision:

Scarlett: *Sometimes you put a form to what you've heard from God and only through going through situations, not being blinkered, you see the need to wait on the Lord for him to open doors in his timing.*

The importance of individuals being open to God's leading was emphasized by Aaron, who gave salutary warnings about both the nature of the error in churches and about the dangerous consequences of leaving a church without God's specific leading:

Aaron: *There is something very wrong, but it's not just one thing. I believe that the Lord is revealing the truth in these days. I believe he is showing to those who are searching what is going on. There is a spirit of error that has infiltrated.*

The Lord will lead us individually into situations where we need to speak out or not, but it needs to be him who is leading. We have to get the hang of doing less, not more. This is where God intervenes and takes us from one thing to another. I had a back accident and couldn't walk for three weeks. That reset everything for me. If one does this, leaving a church or moving into a true church on your own without God's leading, I have a feeling that you might just end up in a vacuum.

Biblical/Theological Influence

A number of leavers revealed concerns over what we might term theology rather than in relation to practical experience. This often related to the beliefs expressed in churches and how consistent these were with Biblical teaching:

Aaron: *Is God doing something new or doing something old? If you look at prophecy, it's one of the things that switched me on. I realized that God is not surprised by anything. God is not continually doing a new thing. What he prophesied in Isaiah was about Jesus. He is not bringing out a New Testament 2. It's like people who believe God has rejected the Jews and changed his mind. People think that God has to speak to us differently, but everything in the word (of God) is quite sufficient. Satan himself is behind this modern gospel of love. They come to Christ on that basis but then want nothing to do with God when something bad happens. God is a god of love, so he wouldn't take my child. There's a lot of this in the church. People accept Christ on a flimsy basis. They believe in another gospel, all under the umbrella of Christianity.*

Max: *Why I left ULC was a kind of disagreement over theology, but now I've left the faith and think that you could call it either way, 'cause obviously none of it* *is true. The reason why I left ULC was basically because I began listening to preaching and I felt like the systematic theology of that preaching was a better way of interpreting the Bible than what was being preached at ULC.*

In my chat with Declan, there was an interesting reflection on the link between the church's practice of baptism and the presentation of the gospel:

Declan: *I think it's wrong the way people are introduced to being saved and being baptized. It's almost as if people are not told the whole story. Do people really understand what baptism is? 'Do you actually realize what you are doing? What is happening to you? Do you realize that you are dying? When you go under that water, you are dead. Do you realize that? When you come out, you are a completely new man.' If it is explained, is it explained properly? It's a different gospel now. One of the things that does make me feel it's not right is we don't preach the fear of God. We talk about Jesus and how nice he is, how he'll look after you and you need him. He'll be your friend, your mate and everything. We don't tell people how powerful he is. We seem to have lost that, but out of fear comes faith.*

We earlier considered what some leavers had to say about poor communication in churches. Some expressed a link between the theological framework of a particular denomination and this poor communication, particularly in relation to views regarding authority and decision-making. For some this created a void:

Josh: *We were very welcoming and gave lots. I tried to dig deeper into thinking processes and why things fell apart and the lack of conversation and communication—just leaving things in a void. On top of my own experiences, there was a way the church thinks may be related to the denominational tenets. It just doesn't feel right. This was layered on to other things that show there's a lot of wrong thinking.*

Spiritual Elements

Some leavers made specific references to the spiritual nature of church experiences. Sometimes this was expressed in terms of a direct spiritual battle faced by an individual:

Yuna: *The enemy was telling me, 'Get out now. Go.' I'm aware of that battle and susceptible to it. I believe it was something evil telling me I was not worthy of this. It didn't want me to get the ministry.*

More frequently, the spiritual battle was seen in sets of circumstances affecting groups of people or the whole church. Patricia outlines a situation where her trust in leadership was undermined by their response in a particular situation:

Patricia: *There had been a move of the Holy Spirit and this person had actually received healing from awful things and suddenly, now that healing had come, this huge attack came. It was like the enemy came and went 'No!' and used people to do it. It just devastated and shipwrecked so many people's faith. It was shocking. It took a while to recover from that and to trust leadership.*

A few leavers expressed concerns that aspects of church theology can sometimes be more than accidentally damaging and may be directly deceptive and largely unchallenged:

Aaron: *This thing called Christianity was not just generally intact with a few loose cannons and wolves. No. It was much, much worse. I really searched for what the truth was. There is a verse saying God sends a great delusion because people are not lovers of the truth. I had not heard all this stuff from the pulpit. They don't talk about the deceptions. Most of the deceiving theology isn't called out.*

Authenticity

Given what Jesus said about the truth setting us free, it is sad to hear the experience of some leavers suggesting that churches can lack honesty or authenticity:

Kaylee: *I'm looking for authenticity. I got a lot of stuff at ULC that was not authentic. I was less and less enraptured by the worship and felt increasingly like a second-class Christian. There is so much overt display of being in the spirit at the expense of being more discrete but powerfully connected to God. It's manipulation.*

Steve: *I got accused of something that made me feel excluded and unwelcome. I thought if one person feels like this, how many other people do? I think one of the biggest things was that two-faced-ness. To be all open and loving in front of people but then make me feel (bad). It was hard to feel if one person could pull the wool over my eyes, how do I feel about the whole church?*

For some leavers, church leaders lose credibility and undermine authenticity through their dishonest public presentation of the reasons why people leave:

Ralph: *There are various reasons why you leave, but they are probably symptoms rather than the cause. It got really frustrating at St. Valerie's... There were* *ridiculous reasons that were made up for why people had left.*

Some leavers express concern about dishonesty in communication where spiritualized language is used to cloak the truth in order to present an interpretation of events that raises fewer unsettling questions:

Morris: *I think that whole 'For a season' thing just seems to be an excuse for either getting rid of someone from something or it being an excuse for why you're stopping doing something. I actually do agree with the concept of doing things for a season, but in my experience, it always seems to have been used as a bit of wallpaper to cover where people don't want you to do something anymore or when someone's made a massive cock-up and 'How do we explain to the congregation that they've got to go without actually ruining their reputation?'*

In some cases, it seems that there is a lack of transparency due to churches wanting to keep up the appearance of a good organization or successful activity:

Agnes: *actually, all you need is for somebody to say, 'We've started to do this, but we don't actually know what we are doing,' or 'This isn't working, so we are going to stop.' It's that transparency.*

On other occasions, the authenticity of beliefs and experience is challenged because it appears irrelevant or trivial in comparison with the most challenging aspects of the human condition:

Max: *I look around the world and I see some of the things that happen like I see kids dying with cancer and then some guy at church says, 'Oh yes, God healed my elbow that was hurt,' or something like that, I think for God's sake! This is typical of places like St. Stephen's— their youth group and stuff like that. They get all excited and they say, 'Oh, I got healed from this and that,' and when I look at the crap that they believe in, I just think they're a joke. None of them know the Bible. None of them are serious. They're all happy-clappy. Oh man, I couldn't stand any of them.*

Authenticity is important for full commitment, and we know that a lack of reality is no basis for the commitment of our time, energies and money.

Change

Some leavers recognize that as they have matured and changed within themselves, their feelings about the church have changed. This can be a drifting apart from the church due to personal changes, as in Ralph's case:

Ralph: *If you assume your relationship with God is just that, a relationship and that you're on a journey, then this means change. It means you will change— your attitudes and aspirations. Strange things can happen as part of the journey.*

We noted earlier that some leavers perceive a change, that as people move from being church joiners to more established members of congregations, the expectations change and there is less concern or forgiveness. However, there can also be a view that the 'diet' no longer meets the nutritional requirements of a more mature believer. David Murrow has interesting light to shed on this phenomenon. In his book *'The Map: The way of all great men,'* he notes how even the best lively modern churches find it much harder to retain well-established attendees than to bring in newcomers *(17)*. He previously gained both popularity and notoriety for explaining *'Why Men Hate Going to Church'* *(18)*, but in *'The Map'* he offers a very enlightening observation that clearly reflects the experience of some leavers regarding the restricted provision in churches that doesn't cater for stages of growth in people's faith and experience. This process of change and growth was well described by Nigel:

Nigel: *You were young in your faith and it was a whole new world opening up to you, but after a while, you then start to grow in your faith then you want more from what you are attending. The bigger picture is actually, could we have tolerated what was going on and stayed where we were, from a Christian perspective, and dealt with it and accepted other people's ways of doing things and decisions that were made, and I think at that stage in our faith was it naïve of us to say, 'No we'll move on?' I don't know.*

PART 3: APPLYING WHAT WE LEARN

Having now tried to identify subjects in focus and thematic presentations of leavers' contributions, you are probably better placed to respond to thoughts and ideas stimulated rather than to be told what to do next.

However, I do believe that any genuinely honest and helpful application of 'learning from leavers' will need to consider several elements. I do not offer these as deeply spiritual principles or coherent strategies. To do either would be beyond the remit of this book and, in all likelihood, beyond my capabilities. These are five suggestions which I tentatively offer and which I will begin exploring over the next few pages as follows:

- Take responsibility

- Listen well

- Seek and speak the truth in love

- Promote unity

- Love, forgive and stay or leave well

Take Responsibility

*Share each other's burdens and in this way obey the
law of Christ. (vs 2)
For we are each responsible for our own conduct. (vs
5)
Whenever we have the opportunity we should do good
to everyone- especially to those in the family of faith.
(vs 10)*

Galatians 6:2-10

Church leaving commonly reveals the tendency,
both within those who leave and those who are left, to
apportion blame to others. It often seems to exhibit a
corresponding failure to accept responsibility for
personal conduct. The acceptance of fractured
relationships must surely demonstrate a lack of
commitment to Christ, who calls us to love one another
and to do so in observable unity so that the world will
recognize who he is (John 13:34-35, 14:15 and 17:21-
23).

Leaders, in whatever model of institutional or non-
institutional church, must step up and take
responsibility for what is happening to both those who
stay and those who leave. It is their responsibility to
ensure that people can either stay well—in love and
unity, or leave well—in love and unity.

Leaders need to take responsibility by educating and enlightening themselves beyond the confines of their existing sectarian or denominational thinking. They need to accept the inevitable risks of leadership, not allowing their own sometimes fragile egos to frame any dissent as spiritual rebellion. But most of all, leaders need to take the responsibility of ensuring that their leadership behaviors follow the teaching and example of Christ—not rooted in hierarchical authority, but in service (Luke 22:25-27).

Leavers have a similar calling of love, to take responsibility for their decisions and to communicate them in the way that best serves the blessing they can be to the church they are leaving and themselves. This blessing may well come in the form of a challenge but when it is spoken in genuine love with the intention of building up others, it is likely to be less damaging than a critical and unforgiving silence. It is certainly better than the character assassinations on both sides that frequently accompany leaving a church.

Listen Well

*Understand this, my dear brothers and sisters: You
must all be quick to listen, slow to speak, and slow to
become angry. Human anger does not produce the
righteousness that God desires ...
But don't just listen to God's word. You must do what
it says. Otherwise you are only fooling yourselves.*

James 1:19-20, 21

We will probably all recognize the advice to be quick
to listen and slow to speak, but how well do we practice
it? The concept of listening to the voices of
stakeholders is now common in both education and
business, but it seldom seems practiced in churches.
Why do churches find this so difficult?

As we saw earlier, there is sometimes a theology
behind not asking based on hierarchical notions of
authority and leadership or on the perception that all
we need to know is revealed by God and that it is
somehow unspiritual to get a 'human level
consultation' going—that listening to leavers is
unnecessary at best and might even be worldly at
worst.

At other times or in other settings, there is
sometimes a personal fragility in leaders that creates
a fear of listening to leavers.

Whatever the cause, it is only by listening well that churches and church leaders will gain an accurate understanding of why people leave.

It is fundamental to love and forgiveness that we are able to actively listen to one another and in order to do so, we need to be willing to ask thoughtful questions. This most basic of communication requirements applies to church leaders and to leavers alike. It is not just a requirement of Christian leadership to become better at listening. We all need to do so if we genuinely love one another, for Christian love puts others first and considers others' needs as of greater concern than our own (Philippians 2:3-11). It is not only in physically dying that we lay down our lives for one another (John 15:13) but in 'dying' to ourselves on a daily and situational basis in obedience to Christ (John 15:14).

Seek and Speak the Truth in Love

*We will speak the truth in love, growing in every way
more and more like Christ who is the head of his body,
the church...
So stop telling lies. Let us tell our neighbours the truth
for we are all parts of the same body ...
Don't use foul or abusive language. Let everything you
say be good and helpful, so that your words will be an
encouragement to those who hear them.*

Ephesians 4:15,25 and 29

Truthfulness, honesty, authenticity and integrity are fundamental aspects of Christian relationships and communication. So are love and edification. So is forgiveness. There is a danger in many churches of promoting the view that love demands withholding the truth or at least only expecting it to be expressed in such gentle terms that it could never hurt or cause offense. This is especially so when leaders, church systems or church practices are being questioned or challenged or when leaders need to challenge others.

There is an equally dangerous view that emphasizes almost brutal honesty at the expense of gentle love. This can be expressed or interpreted as harsh criticism and I'm certain it is that of which I've been guilty many times and it is a tendency that I have struggled with for years. One of the concerns I have had about writing this book and a factor contributing to its delay is the fear that I will give expression to that type of criticism again and that it will hurt others rather than being the cause of them being built up and encouraged.

In seeking the truth, church leaders can greatly benefit their churches by listening, as we have noted. Creating practical opportunities for people to express their views honestly, truthfully, candidly and fully without fear or favor might seem quite a daunting prospect with the concern that it could open up the floodgates of criticism.

In truth, what are the loving and effective alternatives? It is neither wholesome nor safe to allow an atmosphere to persist in which people are only approved or regarded as being 'inside' if they agree all the time or at least never challenge about something concerning them. In the extreme, it is spiritual abuse which has a toxic effect on the life of a church and the lives of the individuals who come under its influence. It is far too common in churches, but it has no place among Christians who are called to live in the truth and walk in the light (1 John 1:5-7).

The adoption of a 'stakeholder views' strategy of regularly receiving, evaluating, and acting on feedback would help churches to identify in advance issues that were rising as common concerns as well as the individual issues not shared by many but worth engaging with or incorporating in the church's evaluation of how things are going.

Simply expressed, my suggested 'practical starter' to better address the church leaving problem is threefold:

1) Everyone involved commits to valuing others in the way Jesus has taught us both through his teaching and his example. Any claim to genuinely loving God involves loving our 'neighbour' as ourselves (the greatest commandment) so we commit to finding ways of working that out in every situation in our relationships with others. This is an exceptionally tough challenge requiring every spiritual resource God has available, but without it other practical strategies are likely to fail.

2) The leaders in churches commit to earnestly and accurately finding out what people think by using a robust process with appropriate communication tools to do so. Such a commitment will involve some serious investigation into which tools will be most helpful and enlightening. A quick homemade questionnaire might be a start, but it is unlikely to reveal much more than the preconceived notions of the mind that designed it!

3) Individuals in churches communicate their concerns or reasons for leaving using the tools provided by church leaders or other reliable sources. If no such tools are available, then some written form of communication is used to convey honestly and lovingly what needs to be said. Wherever possible, this needs to be done before the point of leaving so that a genuine process of communication can be supported.

There is also much to be gained by leaders being consistently truthful in communicating with and about those who leave. There is nothing to be gained except incredulity and increased gossiping by repeated pseudo-spiritual cover-ups when people leave. Most of us are not foolish. We can easily recognize 'spun' explanations about why people have left and if it happens enough, it undermines respect and confidence in the honesty of leadership.

Leavers also need to be honest and not contrive to avoid any suggestion of criticism or put a spiritual 'spin' on their reasons for leaving to present a more acceptable face to others and perhaps make themselves sound less selfish or consumerist. This is especially so if, at the same time, they are bad-mouthing the church and its leaders to all and sundry.

Lest we forget the power of truth:

Jesus said to the people who believed in him, "You are truly my disciples if you remain faithful to my teachings. And you will know the truth, and the truth will set you free."
John 8:31-32

Promote Unity

I am praying not only for these disciples but also for all who will ever believe in me through their message. I pray that they will all be one, just as you and I are one-as you are in me, Father, and I am in you. And may they be in us so that the world will believe you sent me.

John 17:20-21

I appeal to you dear brothers and sisters, by the authority of our Lord Jesus Christ, to live in harmony with each other. Let there be no divisions in the church. Rather, be of one mind, united in thought and purpose ... some of you are saying, "I am a follower of Paul." Others are saying, "I follow Apollos," or "I follow Peter," or "I follow only Christ."
Has Christ been divided into factions? Was I, Paul, crucified for you? Were any of you baptised in the name of Paul? Of course not!
... When one of you says (these things) aren't you acting just like people of the world?

I Corinthians 1:10-13 and 3:4

Christian unity, as we have noted, is much broader and far deeper than unity just within a single church or a denomination. To focus only on unity within a church or a denomination may, in fact, be misleading and is sometimes even spiritually manipulative when it is used as the reason for quashing any dissent in order to achieve what could often be described as uniformity rather than unity.

The sort of unity for which Jesus prayed can never be achieved within a single faction or institution because they already represent the division about which he is so concerned and which Paul clearly saw as worldly. John 17 makes it abundantly clear that the unity between believers is a deep spiritual unity based on the love that Christians have for one another as commanded earlier in John 13. It is not a strategic program, although it definitely requires thoughtful action. Neither is it an ephemeral spiritual reality that makes no observable difference.

If we struggle to grasp how churches, as we know them, can embody the unity for which Jesus prayed and for which Paul contended, then we can at least play our part in working out, in our attitudes and actions, how loving God and one another can be expressed in truthful, supportive, uplifting and sometimes challenging ways that foster a greater experience and expression of Christian unity in any local area or community. We can agree that Christ will build his church universally (Matthew 16:18) but the challenge for most of us is to allow him to do it in and through us locally – right where we are.

Some people, as we have noted, see all institutional churches as part of an apostate church system and regard any attempt to achieve unity as therefore theologically flawed. I have not given up on churches in that way. God is gracious and exceedingly clever. We can see, both biblically and historically, how he is able to work even through those human institutions that exist despite his clearly communicated will to the contrary. We only need to consider the existence of kingship in ancient Israel to know that is the case. He bore the rejection of himself as King (1 Samuel 8) because the people wanted a human king, but he was still involved in the leadership of Israel even to the extent of providing a savior through the line of David, the most famous, and sometimes infamous, king of Israel.

In a similar way I think individual churches, however flawed, can still stand as representations of the true Church in a visible way and that God can increase unity within them and beyond them even if it is despite them! What we desperately need to achieve is a transformation that changes more of them into better such representations. The love evidenced between believers can bear testimony to a deep unity in the body even when we go our different ways if only we can do so well—with grace, forgiveness and blessing. This means that the transformation we may want to see in churches has, first and foremost, to be evident in us as individuals. Now there is a challenge!

I am hoping that what our leavers have to say might stimulate some thoughts of change that will redirect at least a few churches in a new and better way. It is a conversation that needs to be had in which we seek and speak the truth but also one in which we have a shared concern for the unity of believers and the world that is looking on at how we handle the whole business.

Love, Forgive and Stay or Leave Well

'Since God chose you to be the holy people he loves, you must clothe yourselves with tender-hearted mercy, kindness, humility, gentleness and patience. Make allowance for each other's faults, and forgive anyone who offends you. Remember, the Lord forgave you so you must forgive others. Above all, clothe yourselves with love, which binds us all together in perfect harmony.'

Colossians 3:12-14

Staying in the church well can only be achieved if love is the motivation and force at work. Love underpins all the other values and relational aspects that enable diverse people to remain in close fellowship and, crucially, to be able to forgive one another. We need to remember that when a person leaves a church, they are not necessarily leaving Christ or his body, the true Church. Love remains the overriding principle. If that can't be expressed by leaders to leavers or potential leavers, then perhaps the church has failed in the most fundamental of expressions of the Christian community. If love can't be expressed by leavers, then they cannot be said to be leaving well and there is little mitigation to the absence of forgiveness and the pain of separation.

The key responsibility for all Christians involved in church leaving, and that includes leavers, stayers or leaders, is to express love throughout the process –

before, during, after and maybe even instead of leaving. As I have indicated, this includes the practical application of that love. I have suggested that it is necessary for churches to set up processes using appropriate communication tools and resources to enable their people to communicate in honest and loving ways. That's much more than just dishing out exit questionnaires! It also entails a commitment not just to listen but to actively do so and consequently to learn through appropriate analysis and evaluation of what is being heard. This requires a genuine commitment of love, time and attention. Consequently, it is also the responsibility of individuals to use such opportunities for the learning and growth of all.

Whether staying or leaving, we must all remember that where love is the goal, forgiveness is the greatest test of whether such love truly exists. Loving, gracious and honest communication is the greatest test of whether the forgiveness is real.

Let love be our greatest goal

(1 Cor. 14:1a)

PART 4: LEAVERS' POSTSCRIPTS

As part of the original conversations, I had sought permission from each leaver to record our 'chat' and had assured them all that I would seek their explicit permission to use any particular contribution they had made, and in the manner, I had selectively done so. When I sent them the anonymized draft to read, I gave them the opportunity to select an alternative pseudonym if, for any reason, they were unhappy about the selected one. I also gave them the opportunity to respond by way of email comments.

I decided not to incorporate any responses into the original text for several reasons, but the most obvious were the following:

1. They did not form part of the original chat, which captured at the moment in time the perceptions and communications of leavers at that time;

2. The passage of time provides an opportunity to reflect on how experiences since the chats have confirmed or changed perceptions. It could prove very interesting to discover what our leavers think after several years.

I decided to use only what was sent to me in writing and not to add any commentary of my own, preferring rather to let the leavers speak for themselves. I did, however, need to maintain the anonymity that I had established for the sake of confidentiality and coherence.

Postscript to Chat 3: George and Scarlett—God Moves Us On
Scarlett:

It is a sad read that so many are hurt or disillusioned by people or situations that arise from within the Body of Christ. It reminds me that we are a very imperfect people who fail the Lord and our brothers and sisters in Christ on a regular basis. But that even those who have been hurt are equally flawed and prone to act in ways that fail others; we all stand accountable before the Lord.

It is clear that our collective enemy uses our failings to bring about fractures within the body, and we are all at risk of falling into his schemes. I am so thankful that the Lord never lets go of those who are His and is very patient and gentle in His guidance.

Postscript to Chat 4: Jocelyn and Jayden—Zoning Out

Jocelyn:

Thank you for bravely tackling a contentious topic and drawing out key lessons for all on this, especially church leaders. There is a great investment put in at the front door, but the fall out the back doesn't necessarily mean a community is growing as a result.

Well done for exploring why this could be with real-life experiences. It is refreshing to have verbalized the myriad of questions that arise when we bravely critique what church is about and why we even bother.

Being a Christian is about following Christ, but if we are not careful, it becomes about following a church or set of man-ordained rules for the different denominations or a leader with a particular ego or mantra.

I fully accept that for many of us, church muddies the water in how we live out our faith and takes much reflection and energy to sort through God-ordained order over man's institutions.

Being flawed individuals interacting with flawed individuals further complicates the process as God uses individual scenarios to mature us and lead us on. It is odd that sometimes this process calls us out of the established church to hear more clearly the voice of our

Saviour and protect us from the very things instituted to help, but very often do the opposite!

I so appreciated the lockdown. An opportunity to reflect and refocus on what is important. Whilst church has a part to play in our faith, it's more about Jesus and how the local church can facilitate the expression of all He stood for. As a result, I am not so involved. I serve where I can as I believe this is important, but my mission field is those I work with, both patients and colleagues and friends I walk with. I endeavor to live out a life flowing first and foremost from a devotion to Jesus and what He has done for me, not behave in a way the church expects us to and be drawn into making it all about how many church activities I do. This revelation was humbling and brought much repentance. It is sad to think that God is often more at work outside the church than within it! I have often said it is sad that the church thinks it has a monopoly on God. If He can use a donkey He can use anyone, whether in or out of the church! (I assume God using a donkey is a biblical reference to Balaam's donkey in Numbers 25)

Postscript to Chat 5: Ben—Musical Mishaps

As a music team leader, I can remember coming back from several Spring Harvests in the late 80s with 2 or 3 new songs that had been thoughtfully written, were full of biblical references and were pleasingly tuneful. They caught on quickly and many are still around today. Spring Harvest had a good mix of songs from different ages, which seemed to appeal to all age groups.

Sadly, this steady stream of new, meaningful worship songs seems to have accelerated into a flood of ill-conceived, highly-emotional songs that no longer enable the whole congregation to become fully engaged in much of the musical worship on offer in some churches. I can appreciate and worship along with a song that has meaning, expressing coherent biblical truths, even if I don't particularly enjoy the melody, but banal repetition of disconnected phrases, accompanied by deafening music (particularly crashing drums) from a performing band up on a stage above the congregation seems to me to be trying to replicate a rock concert for a very limited audience. I'm not saying that the occasional song like this is wrong to include in service, but the growing practice, it seems to me, is to have several of these often vacuous songs in a prolonged assault on the senses of ordinary worshippers, who really only want to express biblical treasures (and perhaps learn new insights into the Bible itself), surely the bedrock of our faith!

Some churches seem to think that everything has to be new and that traditional songs/hymns have hardly any place in modern worship. By all means have new material, but look to the wealth of wonderful, meaningful songs of praise from the past, which still resonate today.

One church that I attended for a while had a policy of avoiding anything that was more than 6 months old, whilst one poor elderly man I spoke to, who had been attending the church all his life, was driven to waiting in his car outside until the 40 minute worship session was over, before going in! He could obviously hear it from outside in his car! I found it shocking and saddening beyond measure to hear him say, "I hate it!" almost with tears in his eyes

I gave up attending the church because I found myself with a headache every time I went, even though I had rarely experienced headaches in my whole life beforehand! I'd got to the point where almost every time I came out of church I was distressed by the experience and it was invariably the music and worship that was the main cause.

I'm saddened by the growing trend toward performance by the music team, particularly when the music is so loud that it obscures the words and assaults the senses. I found myself increasingly sitting down and trying to read my Bible to blot out the effect the 'worship' was having on me.

*I've noticed that 'Songs of Praise' (a BBC television program) is going the same way, with an ever-growing proportion of the songs being individuals performing as if they were at a concert. Even worse is that the words are often so unintelligible that we have to have the subtitles on to follow what they are singing—how can that be worship? Then, to cap it all, the congregation claps at the end as they if **were** at a concert!*

I can fully appreciate that a congregation would feel it right to clap and cheer exuberantly after a triumphant hymn that has expressed our faith so perfectly, like 'Thank You, Jesus, for the Blood Applied,' but clapping 'a performance' in a worship slot, seems really inappropriate to me.

A little example of that (performance element) was at Upton Hope Church at Christmas. They were singing a song that was banal… I got so disinterested that I was watching the bass player who spent the entire time looking down and fiddling with his instrument controls—on his pedal on the floor, then on the amp behind him. It's not a very good example for people. You're drawn to looking at them and you get distracted.

Postscript to Chat 7: Garth and Yuna—Need To Be There?
Garth:

I would have so much more to say now I'm away from the church for good. Honestly, the connection I have with God is so much more personal now. There was so much prejudice in the church and them selling the actual church building for a greater profit really didn't sit well with me.

Postscript to Chat 8: Ruby—Communication Crisis

You asked me initially, 'I think' why I left or it could have been what was the surrounding issues of my leaving or why do I think the church doesn't react well to people leaving people... I can't remember now. But that isn't the reason I finally left the church.

That's why I asked for another meeting at that time. I was just explaining an overall problem. The real reason I left the church, however (as a whole), wasn't because of awful behavior from leadership but because they lacked any sort of gift of discernment. It's barely visible.

A criminal and sociopath/narcissist was being allowed direct connection with leadership and the church's running and nobody was doing anything about this. I've seen this over and over again in so many churches where the ego is present. No gift of discernment was used. Sadly, that is why I made the decision to leave the church for good.

Postscript to Chat 10: Ralph—All Change

I have read with interest and not a lot that I can relate to in everyone else's story.

I am still living on the fringes. I have neither selected a new Church nor have I returned to the old one. I would say that my relationship with the Lord is okay but could be better! (I imagine we could all say that.) There have been changes in my work life since we met and the way that has developed certainly has God's bootprints all over it. I feel that workwise I am exactly where I am supposed to be and I still feel comfortable with where I am church-wise.

I am so glad that you used the quote from me about Churches thinking up ridiculous explanations as to why people leave. In St. Valerie's (I think you called it), we heard that one church was "sheep rustlers," and another lured people away by deception. One family left as they were known as "church hoppers," and another because they liked to put their hands in the air in worship and we didn't really do that sort of thing!

If Churches are to move on, grow and do a better job, then sometimes the elephant in the room needs to be addressed, and the lessons learned. I think a lot of the related experiences also show that people cannot be treated as commodities or sources of income. Neither can a leader assume that they can make major arbitrary decisions without carrying the congregation with them. We are living in a time when church, and indeed Christianity, is being seen as less relevant. I don't think it will overcome that with loud music and shallow preaching. Maybe we need to get back to the basic Jesus stuff, like feeding the hungry, clothing the poor and looking after widows and orphans, for "whatever you do for one of these..." (Ralph's unfinished quotation here is a reference to Matthew 25:31-46)

Postscript to Chat 13: Aaron—Apostate Church

One of the surprising consequences to me of those leaving the institutionalized church like me was the adverse attitudes and reactions of other believers, including friends and family, to the awakening change in my life.

I haven't always been a lover of the truth, in or out of the church. But now, having so recently awoken to the validity and power of knowing the truth of the Word in my life, I find it shocking and sad to discover that most Christians I speak to have settled for the un-biblical, preferring the majority or the traditional view. Even more disturbing, most are not prepared to come together, to study without prejudice and throw out the errors like the Bereans did in Acts 17:11

One could easily become discouraged by the attitudes of others, and I have been, but I hope through these past years, I have become more merciful, more gracious and more prayerful in my relationships with these others. I have to remember where I've come from.

Jesus promised if we search for the truth, we will find it, but there will be persecution when we do. So, we need to learn to stand firm if we are to 'overcome to the end.'

Postscript to Chat 14: Julian—Evangelical Certainty

Thanks for sending your work. And, yes of course, my bit is fine... 'though I do think you should have prefaced it with:-

"...An exceptionally good-looking, charming, and erudite friend....told me..." (...But it's your project; you decide!)

More seriously, it's a great title— "Learning..." We can learn from all sorts. One can often see God in all sorts:- atheists/apostates/existentialists/gays;... as long as they're being honest and speaking from the heart. (...Seeking...)

Sometimes, the Spirit of Truth hovers around a good agnostic / atheist more than around a complacent evangelical Christian; who's proud to belong to a "Bible believin' Church."

And, although I'm sure we would struggle (...for sure!...) to agree on everything:- I do respect you as, very much, a genuine and honest person. And it's good that you get out into the world/pub and listen to people. (...I remember a Barnado's advert that featured a mixed-up delinquent kid: - and the caption underneath was, "That boy needs a darn good listening to." (... i.e., Not a "talking to"/a lecture/a telling off...) Very often, the quality of our listening might speak louder than our words.

One thing you missed about my "beef" with St Stephens and the like was the perverted/condemnatory/unkind (nay, hateful)/foolish obsession with sexual morality. At the time, I had become a member of Changing Attitudes—an Anglican pressure group lobbying against discrimination against gay priests. And, the fact that a nice, kind, decent Sunday school teacher could be "sacked" when it was discovered that she was "living in sin," i.e., didn't have the requisite certificate to live with the man she loved...! ...Well, that really did (...And still does) gobsmack me. (...The difference now is that I just laugh at high-handed "leadership" behavior; ...Rather than get upset and angry, as I did then... It's their problem!)

I remember saying to you that I'd even heard a notable former head of The Evangelical Alliance, Clive Calver, regretting that the Evangelical wing of the Church had got so hung up on sexual morality.

The other problem I had at the time was that I felt debarred from explaining my views in our church magazine. Previously, I had, over time, contributed a good number of articles—that they were always happy to receive. Now that I wanted to express something more controversial—I was, it seemed, being censored.

It may seem strange. But, at the time, I was so upset/disillusioned/angry that not only did I leave St Stephen's, but I actually felt unable to enter a church (any church) for about a year.

I have, of course, largely forgiven and forgotten. And, nowadays, I'm as liable to roll my eyes or laugh—as to get pointlessly angry.

PART 5: APPENDIX: MEANINGS, METHODS AND ME

Learning From Leavers as a Concept

The words 'Learning from the Leavers' came to me, as I remember, as part of a dream. I immediately had a sense of what it meant relating to the experience of church leavers, probably because a good friend of mine had previously compiled an extensive list of those who, in the last year or so, had left the church we both attended. Learning from leavers is quite a simple idea. It basically suggests that we can all learn something from the experience and perceptions of people who leave churches that historically, and at present, we do not seem to be hearing very well. Such learning involves a willingness to listen carefully and reflect thoughtfully. It is likely to benefit us when responded to appropriately, potentially leading to more positive outcomes for churches and for leavers themselves.

I followed my dream up with many conversations with friends and associates and I read what some serious researchers had to say on the issue of church leaving. I was particularly impressed by Steve Aisthorpe's research and his books referenced earlier. *'The Invisible Church: Learning from the experience of churchless Christians'* and the follow-up *'Rewilding the Church'* are both highly recommended reading for anyone who truly wants to understand the experience of people who leave churches, what that means for churches themselves and some important implications for the future.

The data available to us reveals that in some parts of the world, namely Africa, Asia and Latin America, there has been huge growth in the numbers of Christians and churches, but also that in the 'developed' or 'First World' countries the huge numbers are those leaving many mainline denominational churches. Aisthorpe points out well that the picture is more complex than the 'terminal decline' often suggested by popular media headlines, but the truth is that many people have left churches they once attended, whether or not they are attending elsewhere or have become those who, *'live their lives outside the traditional context of a church congregation'* and have what he calls, *'non-congregational Christian faith.' (19)*

It has not been intended in this book to give the impression that it is only leavers who have something valuable to offer, but it may provide something of a balance in affording a voice to those who, it seems, have not been effectively heard in churches through even a process as limited as the classic exit interview. It could be argued that, by contrast, the voices of leaders and those with recognized authority in churches are heard on a very regular basis – at least every Sunday morning. It is worth noting the significant number of leavers who were not just previously attenders but had been in positions of leadership themselves.

Learning from leavers necessitates an openness to accept that those who leave have something worth sharing that may not already be known. While not necessarily endorsing their perceptions, it accords value to their experiences and the expression of their ideas. It may require a shift in thinking, especially on the part of church leaders, away from common assumptions about church leaving so often based on stereotypes and myths rather than genuine experience or real evidence. Aisthorpe contributes significant insight into the *'myths which masquerade as facts'* and the *'stereotypes, generalizations and prejudice'* that abound in relation to church leaving. *(20)*

It is difficult to untangle the reasons why we so easily slip into accepting myths and stereotypes and in attempting to do so, we need to beware of unwittingly reinforcing another set of them. What seems clear, however, is that people who leave churches are not consistently followed up in a way that suggests continuing care or concern. Sometimes this is because they are stereotypically characterized as uncommitted, divisive or as having damaging opinions or behaviors. Sometimes it is because assumptions are made about their personal circumstances. Whatever the reasons for the existing reluctance to listen to leavers, they do no service to the truth or the powerful learning that could take place if a different attitude could be adopted.

The change of attitude involves reframing a perspective about those who leave and, perhaps, about what it means to belong in the first place. There are huge implications for what we regard as being the church, the family of God, the Body of Christ and so on. This could be a very complex matter, but I hope that by listening to what leavers have had to say through their contributions as recorded in this book, readers will be able to gain something of benefit in terms of attitudes towards leavers and the prompting of positive changes in behavior and actions.

It is my contention that there are great potential benefits for churches and for individuals in adopting the learner's disposition towards leavers and would-be leavers—who realistically could be anyone presently attending! Simplistically put, there is at least a preventative benefit: churches might be better informed in addressing problems before (perhaps that should be BEFORE) people leave, and potential leavers might be able to express their thoughts in ways more conducive to peaceful staying or healthy leaving.

A powerful theme that emerges from the experience of leavers is the overwhelming desire to 'leave well' but a common frustration in feeling that it was not possible to do so and that an unnecessary fracture in relationships has taken place, characterized at best by cool indifference. It is a minority of leavers who view churches as part of 'the harlot church system' and their leaving as obedience to the call of Christ to 'Come away from her my people...' *(21)*, although that view finds expression in a couple of our leavers as you will have seen. By contrast, many leavers feel deeply hurt by the void that seems to open up in relationships with those they had considered family or friends but who now never contact them or even avoid them in passing.

A profound benefit of taking a very different approach to church leaving is the potential for observing the followers of Christ going about life and service in ways that glorify him, are consistent with his heart, obedient to his commands and are demonstrative of his kingdom. It needs to be possible to achieve this while either staying or leaving a particular church but doing so entails rightly understanding what Church really is as the Body of Christ and submitting to his Lordship in our lives through obedience to his will regarding the love and unity of his people. Nowhere is his intent for us so stunningly clarified as in the chapters of John's gospel:

So now I am giving you a new commandment:
Love each other. Just as I have loved you, you should
love each other.
Your love for one another will prove to the world that
you are my disciples...
If you love me, obey my commandments...
Those who accept my commandments and obey them
are the ones who love me...
All who love me will do what I say.
My Father will love them, and we will come and make
our home with each of them. Anyone who does not love
me will not obey me.
And remember, my words are not my own.
What I am telling you is from the Father who sent me.

John 13:34-35, 14:15,21, 23-24 and 17:21-23

The love commanded of us towards one another is not optional for those who truly love Christ and are his disciples (obedient to his discipline). I emphasised earlier that this love represents both a responsibility and an opportunity. It certainly demands that we all do this church staying or leaving a lot better than is often experienced and witnessed.

As I have also stressed, one appropriate expression of that is to commit to listening better. I am hoping and indeed praying that this book and the snapshots of perception contained may be of help to individuals and churches in understanding the wide range of thoughts and feelings experienced by leavers. A better understanding will help to guide some all too necessary changes facilitating yet better listening and better support for staying or leaving well. We don't expect snapshots to deliver all-encompassing truth about the subject they capture, but we can still value what they have to offer. I hope that the 'snapshots of perception' presented earlier have provided you with some fresh insights.

Should I Stay or Should I Go? Personal Confessions.

As I have sat writing this for several years, I have faced a very real dilemma and it is important for me to share it with you. Both my wife and I have experienced local church leaving problems of our own. My wife has not attended, for several years, Upton Life Church (ULC)—the church in town that we had attended together for over ten years. Her experiences at the church and the loveless way she received no contact from the leaders or other significant attendees after a long period of non-attendance deeply hurt her spiritually and emotionally. I continued at ULC as well as helping out occasionally at another more local church, St Philip's. I had not had any direct leading from God about leaving either church. I had previously had responsibilities in both churches and didn't want to end up writing this book as somebody who had just left a church!

My service at ULC faltered soon after my wife stopped attending. The COVID-19 pandemic came along and created what seemed like a natural break for me in which I rarely followed the recorded ULC online services. I preferred participating in the Zoom meetings arranged by St. Philip's. I have continued attending and contributing there subsequently because I have felt a sense of belonging to that small community of believers, despite some significant theological differences.

I continue to pray for the leaders and others at ULC and I do not deliberately withhold myself from caring communication, but I did not leave well. I feared the consequences of initiating another challenging conversation with leaders. Nor was my leaving facilitated well by the church. I've experienced the same lack of concern and communication that my wife suffered.

There's a certain irony in being five years into thinking about and doing the research for this book and over a period of several years facing personally, and in my family, a number of similar painful mental and spiritual disturbances that have hurt many of my own church friends and others who have left already or are considering doing so.

What I can at least say with a clear conscience is that I have not sought to use this project to simply justify my own leaving. I started it long before leaving. If anything, I have been desperately putting the project off, hoping that God would change his mind or that I would realize I had misconstrued his intent! I believe he has tried various encouragements to keep me engaged, but it is the sense of responsibility to those who shared their stories that has finally driven me to the finish line.

Regarding My Methods

As noted earlier, some very impressive research has been done by various individuals and organisations. Aisthorpe's is probably the most extensive and yet accessible presentation of the relevant recent research with a particular emphasis on the situation in the UK. By contrast, my book is a project. I have, nevertheless, tried to achieve a reasonable level of consistency, honesty, fairness and respect in working at it and presenting it.

From the start, I wanted this book to be different from other books I have read on church leaving. Most of them draw in data from a wide geographical area and are presented in such a way as to quote leavers' views only illustratively and quite briefly in support of the author's presentation. I wanted to let this book convey a greater sense of both location and personality. In doing so, I have tried to capture and present more fully the experiences of a number of local people who have left local churches in a local town. It is not usually good practice to include too many long quotations, but the nature of this book absolutely requires it, as I have tried to draw your attention to what leavers shared with us. I made suggestions from my own perspective only in the third section – the summary consideration of what we can learn.

My emphasis on the personal stories of local people shared in conversation supports the twin aspects of location and personality. This is not a quantitative study and numerical data has been studiously avoided. Instead, I have tried to allow personal experience and perception to help us reflect and learn. Initially I decided to use unstructured conversations (which I later called 'chats') to allow the stories and themes to emerge in as natural a way as possible without me guiding or constraining them with questions based on my own preconceived ideas. I tried to let themes emerge through carefully listening to and transcribing the conversations. This enabled me to identify themes both by frequency and force of expression, but it also alerted me to some dangers of categorization. None of this ensures objectivity in my approach. Nor does it ensure that I have accurately represented the perceptions of others. Nearly everyone who took part has been given the opportunity to read and help me edit this work. I hope that goes someway to recommending it as reliable, at least as a representation of their stories and views.

I've called my contributors 'leavers' despite it sounding a little impersonal because that, in some way, is the shared experience underpinning their contribution to this project. Each of them has a life with many more meaningful aspects to it than just their experience of leaving a church. My relationship with some leavers is much closer than with others, but none were strangers to me.

The selection of leavers may represent the weakest aspect of my methodology as I deliberately avoided targeting people on the basis of their perceived likelihood of leaving for given reasons. I was attempting to avoid introducing my own bias at that early stage, but I used no rigorous strategy of avoiding unconscious bias and promoting appropriate variation in my selection of leavers with whom to chat. This has undoubtedly had an impact on the themes that emerged which could help to explain why some themes predictably linked to church leaving are not represented at all while others carry greater force than we would usually expect.

One area where I already know this explains a missing theme is in relation to possible racism. I know a small handful of African, Afro-Caribbean and Asian families left local churches before I engaged in my chats with leavers but I neglected to ask them to contribute to my project. I regret the oversight because it would have given them a voice with which to share a very valuable perspective. In one case it would almost certainly have raised the issue of racial discrimination which would then have been represented in the focus subjects and shared themes.

In retrospect, I believe that my bias-conscious decision not to deliberately include a range of leavers has almost certainly led to less varied representation.

I had originally intended to converse with individuals, but at an early stage, a married couple wanted to chat with me together. That led to several of the chats being with couples and I think this also reflects a dimension of church attendance and leaving that doesn't appear to have been a focus for much research. It certainly turned out to be very relevant to this project and I hope that it sheds a little light on the way some couples experience church and church leaving together.

What Is 'Church' Anyway? Trip-up Terminology

This is a subject where it is so easy to trip-up over terminology that it is helpful to identify what is meant throughout this book. There is likely to be continuing disagreement over the selection of words or phrases in relation to 'church,' but I hope you have found at least some internal consistency within this book.

How have I defined the word 'church?' How is it used in this book? I definitely don't mean simply a particular building, but in order to identify either institutional Christianity (sometimes referred to as 'the church') or a specific group belonging to a denomination or organized institutionally and located in a town, I have used the term 'church' with a small initial 'c' (small 'c') rather than following other writers who have offered us 'congregation,' 'fellowship,' 'assembly,' and even (humorously, if somewhat provocatively) 'the thing we call church.' *(22)*

In referring to the Church Universal, the Body of Christ, the Bride of Christ and the collective People of God transcending location and denomination, I have used Church with an initial capital 'C'. You might also have spotted the phrase 'true Church' in contexts where it seems important to make a particular distinction between 'Church' and 'church.' This

Church (capital 'C') is usually referred to in singular terms to indicate its unity as the body of all Christians, although it can also refer to the local embodiment of it—the assembly of God's people—what the New Testament terms the *ekklesia. (23)*

The common term 'local church' complicates matters because we might think it refers to simply the nearest *ekklesia.* Sadly, the divisions that characterize institutional Christianity throughout the world mean this cannot be the case. Some have suggested using definite and indefinite articles to clarify what we mean, so 'the local Church' would refer to *ekklesia*—a local expression of the Church, whereas 'a local church' would refer to one institutional church (probably meeting in a building that gets identified as the name of the church even where they insist that it's a group of people and not the building!)

As far as I am aware, no such use of capitalization or articles has been agreed upon by all the writers on the subject, so for the sake of an attempt at clarity, the 'churches' described in this book refer to local churches belonging to various denominations. The main meetings tend to be held on Sunday mornings in a building. These churches are institutional. They have recognizable meeting formats, service rotas and structured leadership patterns. Most employ staff and have charity status. These are the churches (small 'c') that our leavers have left. Whether they have left the *ekklesia* or indeed, the Church (capital 'C') is another matter entirely, as has hopefully become apparent.

Does It Matter That People Leave? A Personal Reflection

If you read enough books about the church and people's experiences of churches, it isn't long before you appreciate the range of great inconsistencies and contradictions that exist. The aims and claims of churches are usually full of faith, hope, love and positivity, but the experience of many attendees doesn't match, and they find themselves questioning, as Philip Yancey did, 'Church: Why bother?' *(24)*

In the end, does it really matter that people have difficulties in churches or that they leave, or that they don't go back to them after a global pandemic or a break for some other reason? What is the worst that can happen? Are the consequences any more serious than temporary personal or institutional pain? Isn't it a good thing that many are freeing themselves from the pagan foundations *(25)* of so much of what churches do, especially if they are finding new and vibrant ways of living out their faith, enjoying fellowship and being Church with other believers outside of the institutions?

Despite a range of such possible perspectives, it is my contention that church leaving matters a great deal because of its profound impact on individuals personally, on relationships between people and for what it implies to a watching world about the nature of Christ and his Church.

When people leave churches, there is usually great pain for them and others, and relationships are often ruined or at least fail to be examples of Christian love. To top it all, the watching world doesn't know that what they are seeing isn't necessarily an accurate representation of the true Church, whether universal or local. When they witness loveless church leaving, it only confirms their worst suspicions about hypocritical Christianity and the disunity that characterizes it. Even worse if they know that Jesus said:

May they be brought to complete unity to let the world know that you sent me and have loved them even as you have loved me.

John 17:23

So, in answer to the question—YES. It really does matter and, as I think we have seen, the way it happens matters a great deal. Individual churches only partially represent what Church really is. It ought to be possible to leave a church (not the Church) with sufficient love, grace, forgiveness and truth expressed on both sides that even in leaving, there can be a positive witness to love and unity in the Body of Christ.

If leaving a church is the appropriate thing to happen, then leaving well needs to be the aim of everyone involved. I have confessed that this undoubtedly applies to me.

What about you?

NOTES

1. Avicci and Garrix, 2015, *Waiting for Love*, Universal Music Group N.V.—This was a Progressive House song by Swedish DJ and music producer Avicii, produced by Avicii and Dutch producer Martin Garrix and featuring uncredited vocals from Simon Aldred, who wrote the lyrics. The song gives expression to a fairly common notion expressed in modern lyrics that genuine love is not to be found in church or religion.

2. Virgo, T., 2011, *The Spirit-Filled Church: Finding your place in God's purpose*, Oxford: Monarch Books

3. Scazzero, P., 2017, *Emotionally Healthy Spirituality*, Grand Rapids: Zondervan, p119

4. Watchman Nee, 1982 (from Bible study notes 1934), *The Church and the Work 1: Assembly Life*, CFP

5. Scazzero, P., 2018, *Emotionally Healthy Spirituality Day by Day*, Grand Rapids: Zondervan

6. Nouwen, H., 1991, *In the Name of Jesus: Reflections on Christian Leadership*, New York: Crossroads Publishing

7. Brunner, E., 1952, *The Misunderstanding of the Church*, Lutterworth Press, p107

8. Newbold, C.E., 1999, *The Harlot Church System: "Come out of her, My people"*, Knoxville: Ingathering Press

9. Viola, F. and Barna, G., 2008, *Pagan Christianity? Exploring the Roots of Our Church Practices*, Tyndale

10. Chan, F., 2018, *Letters to the Church*, Colorado Springs: David C Cook

11. Calver, G., 2004, *Disappointed with Jesus? Why do so many young people give up on God?* Oxford: Monarch

12. Grylls, B., 2021, *Never Give Up*, London: Bantam Press / Transworld Publishers

13. Aisthorpe, S., 2016, *The Invisible Church: Learning from the experience of churchless Christians*, Edinburgh: Saint Andrew Press

14. Aisthorpe, S., 2020, *Rewilding the Church*, Edinburgh: Saint Andrew Press.

15. Aisthorpe: S., 2020, Ibid, p202

16. Virgo: Ibid

17.   Murrow, D., 2010, *The Map: The way of all great men*, Nashville: Thomas Nelson

18.   Murrow, D., 2005, *Why Men Hate Going to Church*, Nashville: Thomas Nelson

19.   Aisthorpe, S., 2016, Ibid, p23

20.   Aisthorpe, S., 2016, Ibid, These are two chapter titles.

21.   Newbold, C.E., 1999, Ibid

22.   The various terms, including 'congregation,' 'fellowship,' 'assembly' are widely used. Newbold is, as far as I am aware, the originator of the term 'the thing we call church' which tends to focus thinking on what it may NOT be in fact!

23.   *Ekklesia* (or ecclesia) is a transliteration of the Koine Greek ἐκκλησία, the New Testament word always referring to an assembly of people and not to a place. In English it is the root of such words as ecclesiastical and ecclesiology. Beyond a Christian context it meant a gathering of citizens called out from their homes into some public place, an assembly.

a. In a Christian context it has been used to mean:

• an assembly of Christians gathered for worship/fellowship;

- a group of Christians, who observe their own religious rites, hold their own religious meetings, and manage their own affairs;
- those who, in any given location gather together in the name of Jesus and are united into one body;
- the whole body of Christians scattered throughout the earth;
- the assembly of faithful Christians already dead and received into heaven.

24. Yancey, P., 1998, *Church: Why Bother?* Grand Rapids: Zondervan. Yancy records his personal church experiences and the journey taken in a way that many will recognise.

25. Viola, F. and Barna, G., 2008, *Pagan Christianity? Exploring the Roots of Our Church Practices*, Tyndale

www.ingramcontent.com/pod-product-compliance
Lightning Source LLC
Chambersburg PA
CBHW051056050726
47592CB00002B/552